GEORGIA

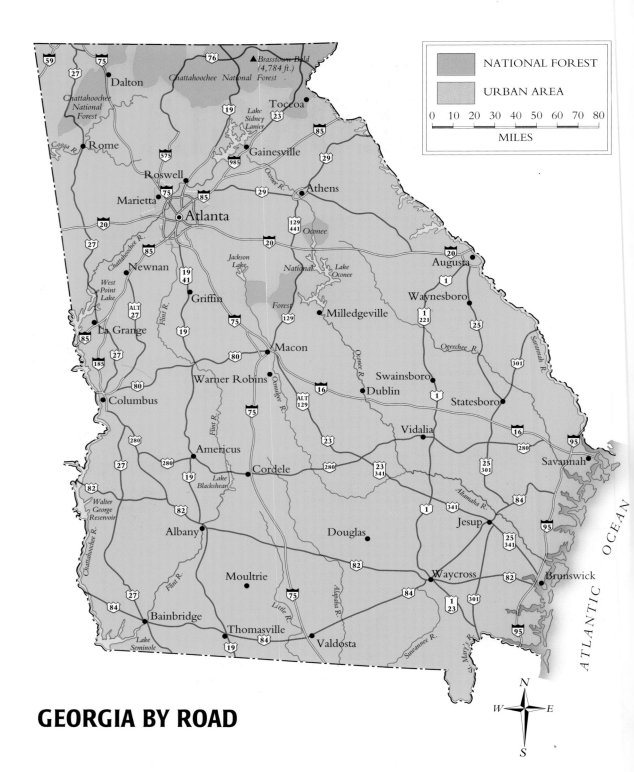

GEORGIA BY ROAD

CELEBRATE THE STATES
GEORGIA

Steve Otfinoski

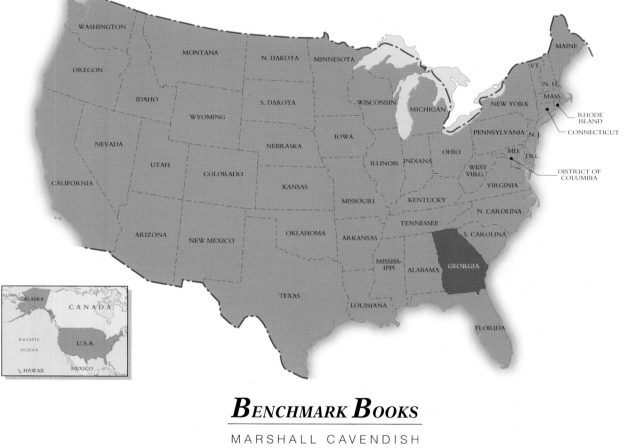

BENCHMARK BOOKS

MARSHALL CAVENDISH
NEW YORK

Benchmark Books
Marshall Cavendish Corporation
99 White Plains Road
Tarrytown, New York 10591-9001

Library of Congress Cataloging-in-Publication Data

Otfinoski, Steven
Georgia / Steve Otfinoski.
p.   cm. — (Celebrate the states)
Includes bibliographical references and index.
Summary: Surveys the geography, history, people, and customs of the state of Georgia.
ISBN 0-7614-1062-7
1. Georgia—Juvenile literature. [1. Georgia.] I. Title. II. Series.
F286.3 .O84   2001   975.8—dc21   99-054073

Photo Research by Candlepants Incorporated

Cover Photo: Corbis/Farrell Grehan

The photographs in this book are used by permission and through the courtesy of; *The Image Bank* : Flip
Chalfant, 6-7; Michael Melford, 113. *Corbis* : 113; David Samuel Robbins, 10-11; Kevin Fleming, 15, 22
(bottom), 55, 58, 64, 78, 101, 102, 124 back cover; Farrell Grehan, 17; David Muench, 20; Raymond
Gehman, 21, 59, 109, 139; Patrick Ward, 24; Richard Cummins, 48-49; Bettmann, 31, 41, 45, 47, 51, 85,
86, 88, 90, 127, 128, 134; Buddy Mays, 54; Bob Krist, 56, 69, 74; Mark Gibson, 57; Joseph Sohm,
Chromosohm Inc., 60, 106; James L. Amos, 66-67, 98-99; Lowell Georgia, 72; Owen Franken, 73, 76;
Richard A. Cooke, 79; Annie Griffiths Belt, 82-83; Flip Schuke, 91; Robert Maass, 95; Tony Roberts, 107;
Stephanie Maze, 112; Kit Kittle, 123; Mitchell Gerber, 125; Ethan Miller, 126 (lower right); Underwood
Underwood, 129; Hulton Duetsch, 130; Neal Preston, 132 (lower); Peter Turnley, 135 (top); Roger Ressmeyer,
135 (lower). *Photo Researchers, Inc.*: Richard Green, 14; Alvin E. Staffan, 22 (top); Farrell Grehan, 114; Dan
Sudia, 117 (top), Douglas Falkner, 120;. *Morris Museum of Art*: 26-27. *Hagrett Rare Book & Manuscript
Library/University of Georgia Libraries*: 29, 33. *Woolaroc Museum Bartlesville, Oklahoma*: 38. *Atlanta History
Center*: 42, William F. Hulk, 81. *Georgia Department of History and Archives*: 43. *Archive Photos*: 126 (top),
132(top); American Stock, 35; Frank Driggs Collection, 93, 131. *Earth Scenes*: John Pontier, 117 (lower).

Printed in Italy

3   5   6   4   2

CONTENTS

GEORGIA IS . . .

Georgia is a state of contrasts . . .

"Here is a land where modern fortresses [Air Force bases] are not far from communities where sacred harpsinging is still carried on . . . a land of forested mountains, deep lakes, and clear mountain streams, contrasted with miles of sunny beaches and sun-drenched isles, with still further contrast in the misty swamps where alligators splash and exotic tropical birds preen their elaborate plumage."

—Former Georgia governor and U.S. president Jimmy Carter

. . . and more than a few surprises.

"Georgia has a lot to offer that may surprise a lot of people. It has a great variety of activities, such as world-class whitewater rivers and great hiking."

—George Whiteley, photographer and outdoorsman

It is a state with a proud and defiant past . . .

"There is no record anywhere that indicates anybody in my family living in 1861 owned slaves. As a matter of fact, I come from a long line of sharecroppers, horse thieves and used car dealers. But a few of them fought anyway—not to keep their slaves, because they didn't have any. I guess they simply thought it was the right thing to do at the time. Whatever the reason, there was a citizenry that once saw fit to fight and die and I come from all that, and I look at those people as brave and gallant, and a frightful force until their hearts and their lands were burnt away."

—Lewis Grizzard, humorist and author

...an exciting present...

"Today, Georgia is a leader. Not just the capital of the New South, but soon to be a capital for the new century."

—Governor Roy Barnes

...and a great future.

"[Atlanta's high technology industry] sounded to me like a glimpse of the future, and I wanted to be a part of it."

—Dannie Gay, electrical engineer

Those who come to Georgia, whether to live or just to visit, never forget it.

"Georgia, Georgia, the whole day through,
Just an old sweet song keeps Georgia on my mind."

—From "Georgia on My Mind," by Hoagy Carmichael

"Georgia on My Mind" is just one of the many songs that have been written about this beautiful southern state. There is something about Georgia's magical land and gracious people that inspires songwriters and everyone else. Georgia is a state that truly stays "on the mind" of anyone who has visited it. Come and meet Georgia.

1 EMPIRE STATE OF THE SOUTH

Georgia is often called the Empire State of the South. Geographically, it is not only the biggest of any state in the South, but of any state east of the Mississippi River. Georgia lies in the very heart of the South and represents everything that is good about the region. From the majestic Appalachian Mountains in the north to the mysterious Okefenokee Swamp in the south, Georgia is a state of great natural beauty.

FROM THE MOUNTAINS TO THE SEA

Georgia is bordered on the north by Tennessee and North Carolina and on the east by South Carolina. Its neighbor to the south is Florida and to the west, Alabama. The state can be divided into three major regions—mountains in the north, a fertile plateau in the center, and an enormous plain that blankets the southern half of the state.

Two important mountain chains end in northern Georgia—the Appalachian and the Blue Ridge Mountains. These are among the most scenic and accessible mountains in the eastern United States. The two-thousand-mile-long Appalachian Trail, a magnet for hikers, ends at Georgia's Springer Mountain. "Hikers starting out here on the Appalachian Trail find it cruel and unusual punishment," says photographer George Whiteley of Atlanta. "From Amicalola Falls

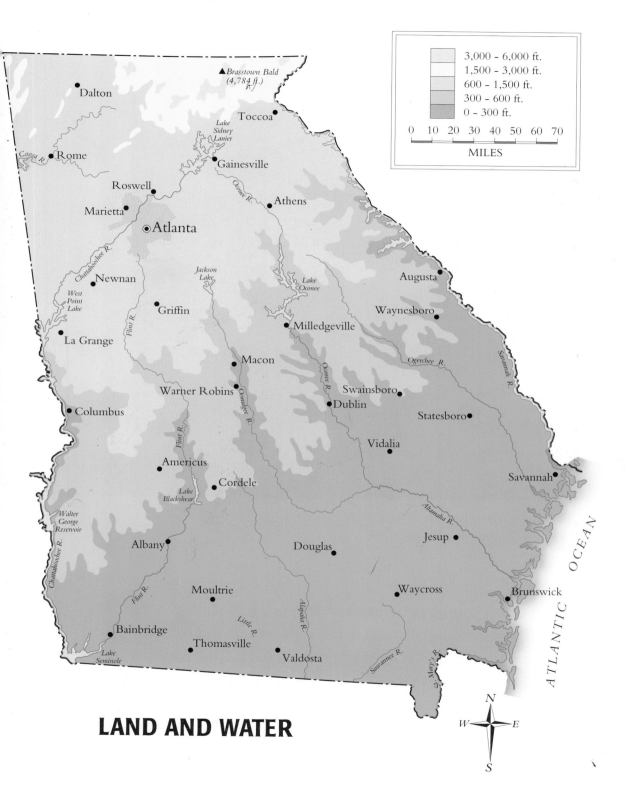

Dalton

▲ *Brasstown Bald*
(4,784 ft.)

Toccoa

Lake Sidney Lanier

Coosa R.

Rome

Gainesville

Roswell

Athens

Marietta

Oconee R.

⊙ Atlanta

Chattahoochee R.

Newnan

Jackson Lake

Lake Oconee

Augusta

West Point Lake

Griffin

Waynesboro

Flint R.

La Grange

Milledgeville

Ogeechee R.

Macon

Oconee R.

Savannah R.

Warner Robins

Swainsboro

Ocmulgee R.

Dublin

Statesboro

Columbus

Americus

Flint R.

Vidalia

Cordele

Lake Blackshear

Savannah

Walter George Reservoir

Altamaha R.

Jesup

Chattahoochee R.

Albany

Douglas

Moultrie

Waycross

Brunswick

Flint R.

Bainbridge

Little R.

Alapaha R.

Lake Seminole

Thomasville

Valdosta

Suwannee R.

St. Mary's R.

ATLANTIC OCEAN

3,000 – 6,000 ft.
1,500 – 3,000 ft.
600 – 1,500 ft.
300 – 600 ft.
0 – 300 ft.

0 10 20 30 40 50 60 70
MILES

N
W   E
S

LAND AND WATER

A spring sunset lights up the rolling ridges of the south Appalachian Mountains in northern Georgia.

State Park to Springer Mountain is straight up." Whiteley's favorite stopping place along the trail is Blood Mountain, one of Georgia's highest peaks. "It was named after a legendary battle between two Cherokee tribes," he explains. "The legend says the warriors' blood ran down the mountain trail." The Chattahoochee National Forest, which includes portions of the two mountain chains, contains Brasstown Bald, Georgia's highest mountain, and Lake Consauga, its highest body of water.

To the south is the Piedmont Plateau, which has rich, red soil and rolling hills. It is the most developed and populated part of the state. Peach trees and tobacco are the most profitable of the many crops Piedmont farmers grow.

This Georgia farm sits in a sea of rich, red soil.

Georgia's many rivers flow into the Atlantic Ocean or the Gulf of Mexico. Many have colorful names, such as Chattahoochee, Oguchee, Ohoopu, and Ocklockmee—reminders of Georgia's rich Native American heritage. Georgia's best-known river is known by the wrong name. Composer Stephen Foster wrote his famous song "Swanee River" about the gentle Suwannee River that runs through Okefenokee Swamp. If Foster misspelled it, maybe it was because he had never seen it, nor even been in Georgia.

Okefenokee Swamp is tucked into the southeastern corner of the state and extends into Florida. The second-largest freshwater swamp in the United States, it abounds with plant and animal life.

The swamp remains a wildlife preserve, but much of the rest of the coastal plain that covers southern Georgia has been turned into farmland. Its sandy soil is perfect for growing such crops as peanuts. Georgia grows more peanuts, which southerners call goobers, than any other state. This accounts for another of its nicknames, the Goober State.

Georgia's one-hundred-mile coast along the Atlantic Ocean is deceptively small. If you were to flatten out all its bays and river mouths and include its offshore islands, it would measure 2,344 miles!

The jewels of Georgia's coast are the Golden Isles. They include Saint Simons, Jekyll, and Sea Islands. While all three lure tourists from near and far, each has its own special attractions. Jekyll Island is a park where visitors can enjoy a wildlife refuge and miles of untouched sandy beaches. Sea Island features a trendy resort for a secluded vacation, while Saint Simons houses the historic ruin of Fort Frederica, built by Georgia's founding father, James Oglethorpe.

OKEFENOKEE SWAMP

The Indians called it Owauquaphenoga, which means "trembling earth." The description is fitting. Much of Okefenokee Swamp is made up of floating islands composed of peat moss. If you stamp on the ground, the trees and plants shake.

But there is nothing impermanent about Georgia's largest swamp. It is a refuge for thousands of birds, animals, and fish. Where the Seminole and Creek Indians once hunted bears, otters, and alligators, these animals are now protected in the Okefenokee National Wildlife Refuge, established in 1937. The refuge takes up much of the 684-square-mile swamp.

Because a lot of the swamp is remote and uninhabited and its old trees and dark water make it seem mysterious, many stories have arisen about it, some going back to the time of the Indians. Encounters with ghosts, the legendary creature known as Bigfoot, and even UFOs have been reported in Okefenokee. No one, however, has sighted perhaps the most famous "residents" of the swamp, cartoonist Walt Kelly's comic strip character Pogo the possum and his friends.

GOOBER PEAS

The diet of soldiers in the Confederate army deteriorated in the declining days of the Civil War. Goober peas are peanuts, which in many cases became the staple food for the rebels—to the point where Georgia soldiers were known as "goober grabbers."

Sit - ting by the road - side On a sum - mer's day,

Chat - ting with my mess - mates, pass - ing time a - way,

Ly - ing in the shad - ow____ un - der - neath the trees,

Good - ness, how de - li - cious,____ eat - ing goob - er peas.

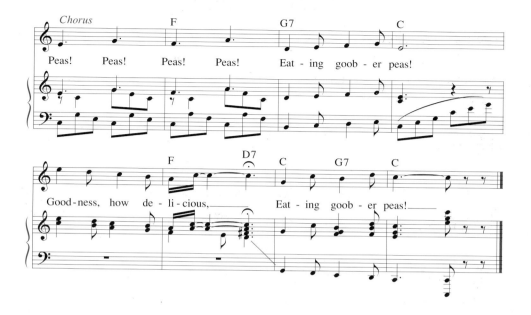

When a horseman passes, the soldiers have a rule,
To cry out at their loudest, "Mister, here's your mule!"
But another pleasure, enchantinger than these,
Is wearing out your grinders, eating goober peas! *Chorus*

Just before the battle the Gen'ral hears a row,
He says, "The Yanks are coming, I hear their rifles now."
He turns around in wonder, and what do you think he sees?
The Georgia Militia—eating goober peas! *Chorus*

I think my song has lasted almost long enough,
The subject's interesting, but rhymes are mighty rough.
I wish this war was over, when free from rags and fleas,
We'd kiss our wives and sweethearts and gobble goober peas. *Chorus*

Georgia's Atlantic coastline boasts sandy beaches and vacation resorts on the nearby Golden Isles.

HOT AND MILD

Most of Georgia has mild winters and hot, humid summers, although cooling summer rains can make the heat more bearable. "I like Georgia in the fall, winter, and spring," says Sue Strickland, who lives in Atlanta. "I don't like Georgia in the summer. It's hot and humid. Then there's the poison ivy and the mosquitoes. They limit my yard work."

The state averages only 1.5 inches of snow a year, usually in the higher elevations. When the odd winter storm strikes the state, traffic is often paralyzed because motorists aren't used to driving in snow and ice. Hurricanes have occasionally swept through the state, but Georgia's coastline has been spared much of the devastation that has struck the coasts of Florida and the Carolinas. Tornadoes are infrequent visitors but can hit hard, as one did in 1986, cutting a destructive path through Cobb County north of Atlanta.

WILD THINGS

The live oak is the state tree of Georgia. The resilience of this majestic tree, which is often festooned with Spanish moss, symbolizes the state's hardy and varied wildlife.

The live oak, Georgia's state tree, grows to an average height of fifty feet and is resistant to insects and diseases.

Muskrats thrive in the swamps of southeastern Georgia. This one is enjoying a meal near some cattails.

The white-tailed deer is also called the Virginia deer, although it is found in Georgia and many other states.

Nearly three-quarters of the state is covered by forest. The sweet-scented pine is the state's most prevalent tree, found in forests in both the north and south. In spring, the woods are alive with gorgeous flowering trees such as magnolia, dogwood, and elderberry.

Each region of the state has its own cherished plants. Laurels and flowering rhododendrons dot the misty mountains. The coastal region is alive with such colorful wildflowers as Japanese honeysuckle and the white-blossomed Cherokee rose, the state flower. Tall saltgrass and cattails bend gracefully in the gentle breezes passing over salt marshes and swamps.

More than nine hundred species of wild animals and birds live in Georgia. Black bears, deer, foxes, and opossums roam the northern mountains, while rivers and swamps abound with muskrats, wild boars, alligators, and a host of snakes, some of them poisonous, such as the coral snake, copperhead, and water moccasin. Birds of every description make their home in such protected refuges as Saint Simons Island and Okefenokee Swamp.

RIVERS AT RISK

Industrial development and population growth, while helping the state's economy, have often hurt its waterways. Georgia's largest city, Atlanta, spills tons of raw sewage into the nearby Chattahoochee River. The city has dragged its feet on sewer construction to solve the problem and has paid out nearly $24 million in fines.

Farther east lies one of Georgia's most popular recreational rivers, the Chattooga, a favorite for canoeists. Developers have bought up 230 acres on both sides of the river along the only major tract on the

Canoeing is a favorite pastime on Georgia's many winding rivers.

river's West Fork that is not part of the Chattahoochee National Forest. The owners claim their stretch of the river is private property and cannot be used for canoeing without permission. A threatening sign that reads Private Property—Survivors Will Be Prosecuted greets paddlers.

The developers say they want to build luxury housing on their land, but many people believe that they are waiting for the National Forest Service to buy the property from them at a profit. Meanwhile, the U.S. Department of Justice is pursuing a lawsuit to declare the West Fork a navigable waterway, which would make it public property. While the negotiations continue, the sign has been taken down.

The Chattooga is just one of the many beautiful rivers in the state that are being preserved, protected, and improved under the River-Care 2000 program, which was launched in 1995 by then governor Zell Miller. In recent years, the state has also added over 100,000 acres to its protected lands, so Georgia's wildlife can have a good home.

2 GEORGIA IN THE MAKING

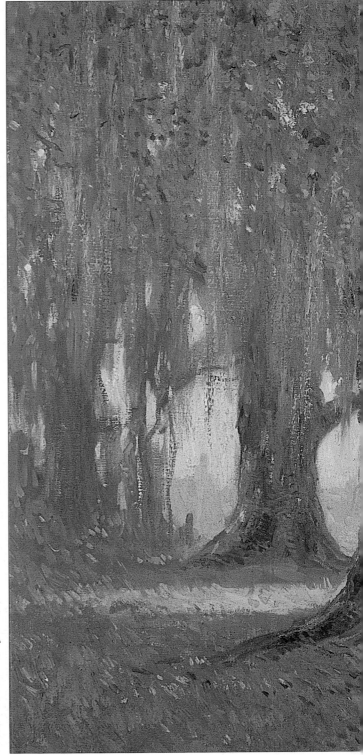

Savannah Oaks, by Eliot Clark

Over its long history Georgia has meant many things to many people. Spanish explorers called conquistadores saw it as a fabled land of gold. British colony builders saw it as a home for Britain's poor and needy. Later, wealthy farmers saw it as a promised land of prosperity and easy living. The African-American slaves who worked their plantations had a very different opinion of the state. Through good times and bad, Georgians have shown a remarkable ability to rise above their troubles, to reinvent themselves, and to snatch triumph from tragedy.

CREEKS AND CHEROKEES

The first inhabitants of present-day Georgia hunted large animals about 11,000 years ago. As time went on, they settled in villages and grew plants for food. They made pottery, the first in North America, about 2500 B.C. By about A.D. 1000, the people in Georgia were building large ceremonial centers with earthen mounds, some as high as sixty feet. What exactly these mounds were used for remains something of a mystery. They may have been places of worship.

About this time, other Native American peoples entered what is now Georgia. The Cherokees, whose name means "cave people," came from the north. The Creeks, named so by English settlers because they often settled alongside streams, came from the southeast.

In addition to the Cherokees and the Creeks, the Yamacraws also lived in Georgia. This is a portrait of Tomochichi, the Yamacraw chief in the 1730s.

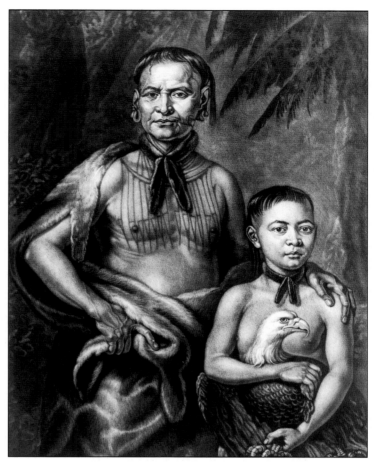

Both tribes were skillful farmers and hunters. They raised corn, squash, beans, and pumpkins. In the forests, they hunted deer and bear and caught fish and turtles in the streams and rivers. Some of the fifty Creek towns had a population of one thousand. Each town had a plaza used for religious ceremonies and games. Houses with roofs made of wood shingles or grass surrounded the plaza. Although living in different regions, the Creeks and Cherokees clashed over land boundaries. These disputes were sometimes settled peaceably by a ball game rather than warfare.

CONQUISTADORES AND PIRATES

The Indians' first encounters with European explorers were not pleasant. Spanish conquistador Hernando de Soto landed in the Spanish colony of Florida in 1539 and marched north with six hundred soldiers. De Soto had been among a party that had found a wealth of gold in Peru in South America a few years earlier. De Soto hoped to do the same in North America. He entered what is now Georgia in 1540. At first the Creeks were friendly to the strangers, but the Spaniards' cruelty soon hardened the Indians.

De Soto's party crossed the Savannah River and continued north where they found pearls and copper, but no gold. Frustrated, but persistent, de Soto headed farther north into the Carolinas. Exhausted and sick with fever, he died on the banks of the Mississippi River in 1542. His men buried him secretly on the river bottom at night. They feared the Indians would attack if they knew their leader was dead.

De Soto's expedition was a disaster, but the Spaniards did not give up on Georgia. It may have had no gold, but its location, just north of their Florida colony, was important strategically. In 1566, Pedro Menéndez de Avilés established the first Spanish fort and mission in Georgia on Saint Catherines Island. Other outposts quickly followed along the Georgia coast. They were meant to defend Georgia against the French, who had established their own colony in Florida in 1564. Within a century, most of the Spanish forts and missions had been abandoned, the inhabitants driven out by the British and their Creek and Cherokee allies.

In the late 1600s and early 1700s, Georgia waters became a favorite haunt for notorious pirates such as Edward Teach, better known as Blackbeard. To this day, some fortune hunters believe the pirate's treasure lies buried somewhere on Blackbeard Island, his headquarters on the Georgia coast.

THE GROWING COLONY

In the early 1700s, Georgia remained a kind of no-man's-land between the British colonies to the north and Spanish Florida to the south. Its fate was altered forever by an English aristocrat with a

The notorious pirate Blackbeard roamed the Georgia coast in the early 1700s. His name came "from that large quantity of hair, which like a frightful meteor, covered his whole face, and frightn'd America, more than any comet that has appear'd there a long time," wrote Captain Charles Johnson in The General History of the Pyrates.

social conscience—James Edward Oglethorpe. Oglethorpe represented a group of men who wanted to help the English poor, especially those condemned to debtors' prison, where people who couldn't pay their debts were confined. In 1730, they asked King George II for land in North America where such unfortunate people could start a new life. George was impressed for two reasons—the new colony would be named Georgia in his honor, and it would provide a strategic buffer between the English Carolinas and Spanish Florida. In 1732, Oglethorpe and thirty-five hardworking but needy families sailed for North America.

After reaching South Carolina, Oglethorpe traveled up the Savannah River in a small boat. "I fixed upon a healthy situation about ten miles from the sea," he wrote to the king. "The river here forms a half-moon, along the south side of which the banks are about forty foot high, and on the top flat." There, Oglethorpe laid out the town of Savannah. One contemporary city planner has called Savannah "one of the finest diagrams for city organization and growth in existence."

Savannah and the colony that grew up around it were to be, in Oglethorpe's words, "a model of virtue." Slavery was not allowed as it was in other English colonies, and liquor was forbidden. There was freedom of worship for Protestants. Each settler would receive fifty acres of land to farm. This generous offer brought several thousand settlers to the colony over the next two decades. They came from not only England but also from Scotland, Germany, Switzerland, and Italy. A group of Jewish immigrants arrived in 1733 and established the third-oldest Jewish congregation in the Americas.

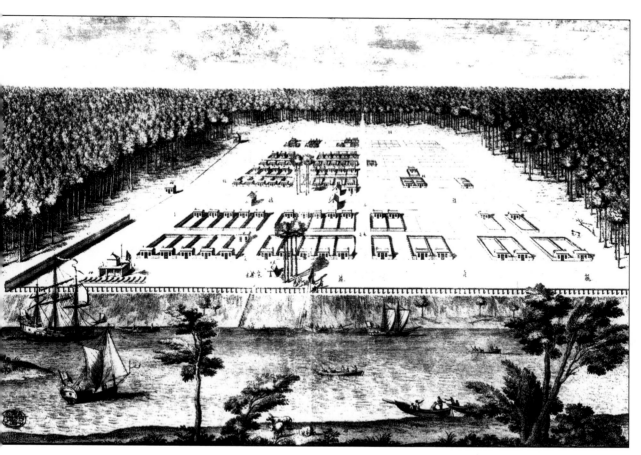

Savannah, Georgia's first settlement, was laid out with ordered precision.

Such growth alarmed the Spaniards in Florida, who went to war against the British colony in 1739. Oglethorpe proved to be as fine a military leader as he was a colony builder. He boldly led his militia in a siege on Saint Augustine, the Spanish stronghold in Florida. Two years later the Spaniards launched a sea attack on Britain's Fort Frederica on Saint Simons Island. The Spaniards far outnumbered the British forces, and feeling confident, they stopped to have lunch in a grassy marsh on the island. But they were surprised by Scottish troops in what has come to be called the Battle of Bloody Marsh. The battle was minor but decisive; the Spaniards were never again a threat to the British in North America, although they held on to Florida until 1819.

By 1740, Georgia was well established as a colony, but it was not to remain the model of virtue that its founder envisioned. While many people in England praised Oglethorpe as the Father of Georgia, many disgruntled settlers called him Our Perpetual Dictator. They wanted to enlarge their farms, and for that they needed the cheap labor that slavery could provide. In 1743, Oglethorpe left Georgia and returned to England. Seven years later, the colony's trustees reluctantly allowed slavery.

Georgia's farms produced rice, indigo, hogs, cotton, and tobacco, and Georgia grew. By 1776, the colony's population was 40,000, nearly half of whom were black slaves.

LOYALISTS AND PATRIOTS

Georgia landowners owed much of their wealth to their trade with England, so when northern colonies talked of revolution in the 1770s, most Georgians opposed the idea. Some would remain Loyalists—active supporters of the king—throughout the Revolutionary War. But when Savannah was attacked by British warships in March 1776, many Georgians were forced to choose sides and join the fight. In December 1778, the British took Savannah. The city would remain in British hands until troops led by General "Mad" Anthony Wayne drove out the enemy in July 1782. A year later the war ended, and the colonies were free.

COTTON IS KING

The war had left Georgia devastated. Georgians who fought on the American side were given free land by the state government. New immigrants were also welcomed, causing a second influx of people from other states and Europe.

Among the newcomers to Georgia was a young man from Connecticut, Eli Whitney, who arrived in Savannah in 1793. Whitney came to Georgia to work as a schoolteacher, but he was also an inventor. "I heard much said of the extreme difficulty of ginning cotton [clearing cotton bolls of seeds]," he wrote in a letter to his parents, "and struck at a plan, a machine with which one man will

Eli Whitney's cotton gin greatly increased the production of cotton in the South, especially in Georgia.

COTTON-PICKING FOLKLORE

Cotton was an integral part of the life on Georgia plantations in the 1800s. In the black community, much folklore grew up around cotton and its magical properties. Here are a few of these superstitions:

If a newly married couple sleeps on a cotton mattress on their wedding night, they will always have money.

If the same couple finds a twin cotton boll, they will have twins within the year.

If an unmarried girl finds a twin cotton boll, she will soon be asked to marry.

When fishing, place twenty dried cottonseeds at the water's edge to guarantee a good catch.

Not all cotton folklore was pure imagination. African Americans' use of cotton as a folk medicine for toothaches, headaches, and other ailments was based on scientific fact. Gossypol, a poisonous yellow pigment in cotton, has some medicinal properties when used in small doses. Large doses can be deadly, however, and some animals have died after eating cotton bolls.

clean ten times as much cotton as he can in any other way."

Whitney's cotton gin was a boon for the South. Cotton could be cleaned much faster than it had been by hand, and it quickly became the principal crop of Georgia and other Southern states. Cotton plantations grew larger, and so did the number of slaves needed to pick cotton in the fields. By the 1820s, Georgia was the world's largest grower of cotton.

But this newfound prosperity was not shared by everyone. For two groups—African-American slaves and Native Americans—it only meant more trouble. The Creeks and Cherokees had adapted well to the ways of the white people, but now they stood in the way of "progress." The government wanted their remaining lands for settlement. In 1825, the Creeks were forced to give up their land and move to Arkansas. Then, in June 1838, soldiers forced the Cherokees off their land. One soldier described rounding up the Cherokees:

> Two or three [Cherokees] dropped their hoes and ran as fast as they could when they saw the soldiers coming into the fields. . . . Chickens, cats, and dogs all ran away when they saw us. Ponies under the shade trees fighting the flies with the noise of their bells; the cows and calves lowing to each other; the poor dogs howling for their owners; the open doors of the cabins as we left them— to have seen it all would have melted to tenderness a heart of stone.

The Cherokees were forced west to Indian Territory, which later became the state of Oklahoma. The thousand-mile journey took six torturous months. Nearly a quarter of the 14,000 Cherokees died along the way from exposure and exhaustion. The route became known as the Trail of Tears.

THE CIVIL WAR

By 1860, Georgia was home to 460,000 slaves—nearly eight times the number in 1800. Although more than half of all farmers had no slaves, the slave system was the backbone of the cotton industry.

The Cherokees called their forced march from Georgia to present-day Oklahoma nuna da ut sun y, *which means "the place where they cried."*

That same year, Abraham Lincoln, a Northerner and member of the Republican Party, was elected president. Lincoln opposed slavery, although he did not immediately seek to abolish it. Southerners were afraid of what Lincoln might do to change their way of life. It was not simply the issue of slavery that mattered, but the right of states to do what they wanted without the interference of the federal government. Southern states began seceding, or breaking away, from the Union. On January 19, 1861, Georgia became the fifth state to

AMERICA'S FIRST GOLD RUSH

Twenty years before the California gold rush sent thousands of Americans to seek their fortune on the West Coast, America's first gold rush took place near Dahlonega, a town in northwestern Georgia.

The discovery was made by Benjamin Parks, who found gold in an overturned rock while deer hunting in 1828. Gold was so plentiful at Dahlonega that in 1838 a federal mint was built there to produce gold coins. Between 1828 and 1848 more than $36 million in gold was mined in the area. The mint shut down at the start of the Civil War, but gold continued to be mined at Dahlonega until the early 1900s.

Dahlonega gold coins are highly prized by collectors, but perhaps the most appreciated gold from the mines is found in the gold leaf on the capitol dome in Atlanta. In 1958, residents donated their gold to re-cover the dome.

Although the days of the first American gold rush are long gone, tourism keeps the memories alive. Visitors to Dahlonega can tour an old gold mine and stamping mill, look through a museum dedicated to the gold rush days, and even pan for gold at a park at the Consolidated Gold Mine. Those who don't find any gold nuggets can always buy one or two at a gift shop.

secede. These states formed their own union, the Confederate States of America, and elected Jefferson Davis as their president and Georgian Alexander H. Stephens as their vice president. Ironically, Stephens, a former congressman, had previously spoken strongly against seceding.

The Civil War erupted in April 1861 when a Confederate militia attacked a federal fort in South Carolina's Charleston Harbor. Georgia played an important role in the war, supplying about 120,000 Confederate soldiers. One of the most industrialized of the Southern states, Georgia's factories supplied the Confederate army with much-needed wagons, clothing, and other goods. Atlanta, established in 1837, had grown into a major city by the Civil War. Its many railroad lines made it a transportation hub for the Confederacy.

Georgia saw little action in the first two years of the war, but in September 1863, Confederates won an important victory at the Battle of Chickamauga. As the war continued, however, the South saw fewer and fewer such victories. General William Tecumseh Sherman lay siege to Atlanta in the summer of 1864. After six months of fighting, Confederate troops abandoned the city, and Sherman burned it to the ground. According to a twenty-eight-year-old Union captain, James Royal Ladd, "the whole business portion of the city was in flames, and notwithstanding the night was dark the blaze illuminated the country for miles."

Sherman proceeded to march from Atlanta toward the coast. His "march to the sea" ended six weeks later in Savannah. Sherman's troops had destroyed everything in their path—farms, towns, and railroad tracks. They had effectively torn the South in two and weakened the will of the Southern people to continue fighting. The war ended the following spring in Union victory.

RECONSTRUCTION

Georgia, like other Confederate states, was occupied by Union troops during the postwar period known as Reconstruction. Northern

General William Tecumseh Sherman and his troops destroyed everything in their path, including railroad tracks, as they marched across Georgia.

opportunists, called carpetbaggers because they carried their belongings in cheap carpetbags, took advantage of the situation to control the state government. African Americans, now freed from slavery, were given the right to vote and run for public office. Resentful white

Georgians joined a secret organization called the Ku Klux Klan (KKK), meant to instill fear into African Americans and outsiders. Although slavery had ended, racism had not. Many African Americans, persecuted and unable to make a living by farming, moved to Northern cities where industrial jobs were more plentiful.

Atlanta was rebuilt and became the state capital in 1868. It was the site of a world's fair in 1881 and was called the showcase of the New South, because it could compete with the industrialized North.

NEW SOUTH, OLD PROBLEMS

The economy of the New South, like that of the Old South, was built on cotton. African Americans and many poor whites became

Atlanta became the showcase of the New South after the Civil War. The Cotton States and International Exhibition of 1895 is just one of a number of fairs held in the city during the late 1800s.

Black sharecroppers pose with a white landowner in this picture taken in Gwinnett County around 1910.

part of the sharecropper system, whereby they were hired to work the land for landowners who would give them a share of the profits. But many landowners took advantage of their workers. Here, a black sharecropper named Ed recalls his experiences in the early 1900s:

> Mr. Prince [landowner] said he'd loan me ten dollars a month. . . . Then, on shares, the boss furnish you with the land, mule, seeds, tools, and one half of the fertilizer. . . .

Things went all right for a while. I was the best cotton picker there. . . . But hard work didn't get me nowhere. Mr. Prince wouldn't show me the papers the gin and the warehouse give him, so I didn't know what the crop had brung and what my share should be. He took his share and all of mine and claim I owe him twenty-four dollars in addition.

But Georgia's landowners and cotton farmers were about to take a fall. In 1895, the price of cotton plummeted. Farmers started growing other crops, such as pecans and peaches, along with cotton, to make a living. By the 1920s, they faced another problem. An insect called the boll weevil had invaded the South, eating cotton bolls and destroying much of their crop. Georgia's economy grew still worse when the Great Depression struck in the 1930s.

Georgia remained one of the poorest states through the first half of the twentieth century. Black Georgians stayed at the bottom of the social and economic order, held back by segregation, the separation of black and white people in housing, in jobs, and at public facilities such as restrooms, drinking fountains, and swimming pools. However, some white Georgians boldly stood up against racial injustice. In the 1940s, prosecutor Lawrence D. Duke won the conviction of two white Klansmen for flogging a black man who later died from his injuries. Governor Eugene Talmadge announced he would grant clemency to the two killers. Duke was enraged and went to a public hearing, which the governor was attending, carrying a whip. Duke held the whip up to the governor's face and denounced the plan. Shortly after, Talmadge reversed his decision, and the killers went to prison.

Other people in public office were trying to improve life in

Prosecutor Lawrence D. Duke confronts Governor Eugene Talmadge with the symbol of racism, a whip, in November 1941. Duke earlier accused the Ku Klux Klan of "systematically . . . carrying out a policy designed to violate the rights of Georgia citizens."

Georgia. Governor Ellis Arnall, who took office in 1943, cleaned up corruption in state government and ended the poll tax that kept black Georgians from voting.

MODERN TIMES

Georgia's economy got a big boost during World War II as local defense plants and other manufacturers hired thousands of workers to meet the demand for wartime production. The 1950s was a time of great change. Northern companies started moving south to take advantage of the warm climate, lower taxes, and large labor force. More and more Georgians were leaving farms and rural areas to find better-paying jobs in towns and cities. In 1960, manufacturing employed more people in Georgia than agriculture for the first time.

This same era saw the birth of the civil rights movement as African Americans and some whites who supported them protested peacefully in marches, sit-ins, and other demonstrations to demand their full rights as citizens. The movement was led by the Reverend Martin Luther King Jr., who was raised in Atlanta. The violent reaction of police and racist groups to these nonviolent protests drew national attention to the civil rights movement and led to the enactment of new federal laws against segregation.

Having won their right to vote, black Georgians began voting African Americans into office. In 1965, Julian Bond, a civil rights leader, was elected to the state house of representatives. Other representatives, however, refused to allow Bond to be seated, because he opposed the Vietnam War. The Supreme Court found the action illegal, and Bond served for ten years in the house before being elected to the state senate. In 1972, Andrew Young became the first black U.S. congressman from Georgia since Reconstruction. Maynard H. Jackson Jr. was elected mayor of Atlanta in 1973, becoming the first black mayor of a large southern city.

Some white racists responded to the civil rights movement of the 1960s by burning down African-American churches.

Today, Georgia can truly call itself the Empire State of the South. In 1996, Atlanta played host to the world at the summer Olympic Games. It was a shining moment for a city and a state that continues to look to a better and brighter future.

3 WORKING TOGETHER

The capitol in Atlanta

Over the years, Georgia has had its political ups and downs. In the past, the issue of race has divided people more often than it has united them. Corruption has sometimes been a problem in state politics. But Georgia also has a tradition of reform and innovation. In 1922, Rebecca L. Fenton of Georgia became the first woman U.S. senator. In 1943, Georgia became the first state to grant the right to vote to eighteen-year-olds. After a century of segregation, black voters have become more powerful, electing to office both blacks and whites who have their best interests at heart.

INSIDE GOVERNMENT

Georgia's government, like every state's, is divided into three branches: executive, legislative, and judicial.

Executive. The chief executive of Georgia is the governor, who is elected to a four-year term. The governor makes appointments to state boards and agencies, proposes the state's budget, and approves or vetoes (rejects) laws made by the state legislature. The legislature can override the veto if two-thirds of each house agrees.

Legislative. Georgia's legislative branch is called the general assembly and consists of two houses—a senate with 56 members and a house of representatives with 180 members. Members of both houses are elected to two-year terms. The legislature works on

Rebecca Felton was appointed to the U.S. Senate in 1922, becoming the first woman to serve in that body. She fought for prison reform and better government.

new laws and helps the governor work out the state budget each year.

Judicial. Georgia's highest court is the state supreme court. Its seven justices are elected for six-year terms. The supreme court evaluates whether laws violate the state constitution and whether cases from lower courts were properly handled. The next highest court is the court of appeals, which reviews cases where the losing side questions a lower court's ruling. Its members are also elected for six-year terms. Judges on superior courts, which hear many kinds of criminal and civil cases, serve four-year elected terms.

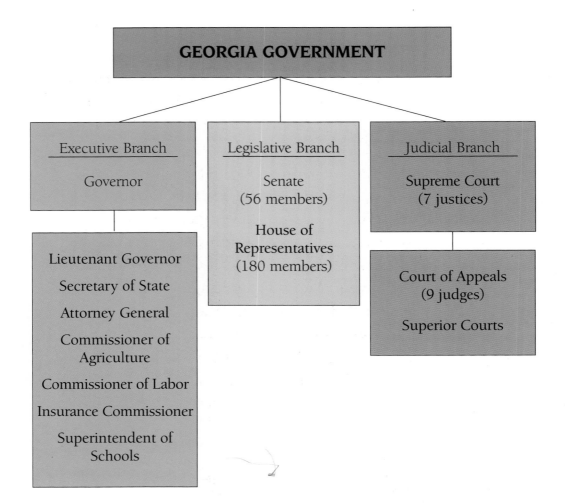

GEORGIA GOVERNMENT

Executive Branch

Governor

Lieutenant Governor

Secretary of State

Attorney General

Commissioner of Agriculture

Commissioner of Labor

Insurance Commissioner

Superintendent of Schools

Legislative Branch

Senate
(56 members)

House of Representatives
(180 members)

Judicial Branch

Supreme Court
(7 justices)

Court of Appeals
(9 judges)

Superior Courts

GUN CONTROL

The right to bear arms is a popular cry in Georgia. The National Rifle Association (NRA) claims to have 90,000 members in the state. But the tide against gun control may be turning. Atlanta, which has a high crime rate, was one of twenty-eight American cities that sued the gun industry in 1999 for failure to install adequate warnings or safety devices on their firearms. The NRA, together with gun companies, countered by lobbying to make such lawsuits illegal. "Georgia is a strong Second-Amendment state," claims Republican state senator Eric Johnson. "People here see any attempt to sue gun manufacturers as an attempt to restrict the citizens' right to keep and bear arms." However, in October 1999 a Georgia judge ruled that a city could sue gun manufacturers.

An organization called Georgians Against Gun Violence is lobbying for a waiting period for buying guns and background checks on potential gun buyers. A five-day waiting period on handgun purchases was abolished by the Georgia legislature in the mid-1990s. Concerned about the number of shootings involving young people, the group says, "It is time for the Republican leadership to stand up to the gun lobby and put America's children first for a change." In January 2000, several state senators introduced the

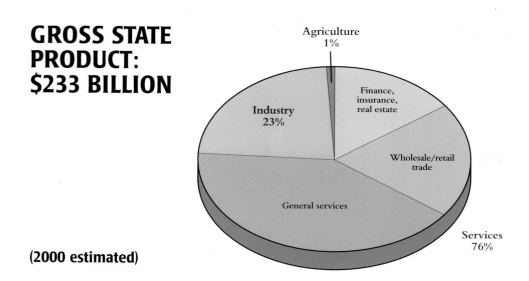

GROSS STATE PRODUCT: $233 BILLION

Agriculture
1%

Finance, insurance, real estate

Industry
23%

Wholesale/retail trade

General services

Services
76%

(2000 estimated)

Child Access Prevention Bill that would make it unlawful to allow minors to possess a pistol or revolver.

THE ECONOMY

Georgia's economy has changed drastically in the last century. In 1900, agriculture drove the economy. Today, most workers are employed in the service sector, including tourism and the computer industry, wholesale and retail trade, and the government. Less than 3 percent of Georgia's workers are employed in agriculture.

Old mansions like this one are important tourist attractions in Georgia today.

THE ONION STATE?

When people think of Georgia they imagine tasty peanuts, juicy peaches, or plump pecans. But sweet onions? Unlikely! Before you turn up your nose at Georgia onions, however, consider those grown in Vidalia, in the southeastern part of the state.

Vidalia onions have been called the "caviar of onions." Unlike other onions, they are sweet, not bitter. They are so sweet that people eat them raw in sandwiches or chop them up to put into marmalade.

Onions weren't always so highly prized in Georgia. Georgia farmers had first noticed the onions' unique flavor in the 1930s, but it wasn't until 1974 that they really became popular. That year Delbert Bland talked his father into replacing their failed tomato crop with onions. Through clever marketing and hard work, Bland made Vidalia onions famous and turned the family onion farm into an international business with more than 125 employees. Today, more than 150 onion growers work in the region.

And what makes Vidalia onions so sweet? Experts say the sweet taste comes from the low sulfur content of southeastern Georgia's sandy soil.

PEANUT BUTTER CORN MUFFINS

Georgians use peanuts in just about everything. And why not? They have so many of them! Have an adult help you make this delicious treat that will enliven any meal.

¾ cup flour
1½ cups cornmeal
4 teaspoons baking powder
1 teaspoon salt
2 eggs, beaten
1¼ cups milk
¼ cup salad oil
jar of crunchy peanut butter

Put the flour, cornmeal, baking powder, and salt into a mixing bowl and blend with an electric mixer. Add eggs, milk, and salad oil to the mixture and blend until smooth.

Put 2 tablespoons of the mixture into the bottom of each cup of a greased muffin pan. Add 1 tablespoon of crunchy peanut butter. Add the remaining mixture to fill each cup.

Bake in a 400-degree oven for 30 minutes. Allow to cool and then dig in!

These children are watching a farmer harvest tobacco, one of Georgia's leading crops.

That doesn't mean farming is no longer important, however. Georgia is number one among the states in the production of peanuts, pecans, lima beans, and pimiento peppers. So many peaches are grown in Georgia that it is nicknamed the Peach State, and many streets in Atlanta and elsewhere contain the word *peach*. Other important crops include wheat, soybeans, tobacco, and, of course, cotton. The state also ranks first in the production of young chickens raised for eating, known as broilers. Other chickens are raised for laying eggs, another important farm product in Georgia.

By comparison, fishing is a modest industry in Georgia and consists mainly of such shellfish as crabs, shrimps, and oysters. Brunswick, in the southeast corner of the state, is one of the South's most important seafood processing centers.

Georgia's pine forests are the mainstay of a thriving lumber industry. The state is the biggest producer of lumber and wood pulp east of the Mississippi. It also ranks first in the nation in the production of turpentine, a liquid from pine trees used in making disinfectants, insecticides, and other chemical products.

Shellfish are the main catch along Georgia's coast.

At pulp mills like this one, wood from Georgia's trees is turned into pulp, which is used to make paper and cardboard.

Mining is less important, although Georgia produces more granite than any other state. Georgia granite has been a popular building material since it was used in the construction of the U.S. Capitol in Washington, D.C. Marble is another popular material used in making buildings, monuments, and gravestones. But perhaps Georgia's most valuable mineral is a rare kind of white clay called kaolin which is dug out of large pits located near the cities of Augusta and Macon. Kaolin is a key ingredient in paint, plastics, rubber, and paper.

Atlanta is the world headquarters for the Coca-Cola Company.

Textiles are Georgia's leading manufactured product. Textile mills in Augusta, Columbus, and elsewhere produce such varied materials as corduroy, terry cloth, and velvet. Dalton, in northern Georgia, produces more than half of the world's tufted carpets. Food processing and automobile and aircraft manufacturing are also important in Georgia.

The business most closely associated with Georgia is the Coca-Cola Company, headquartered in Atlanta. Coke is the most popular soft drink in the world. The beverage was first concocted in a brass

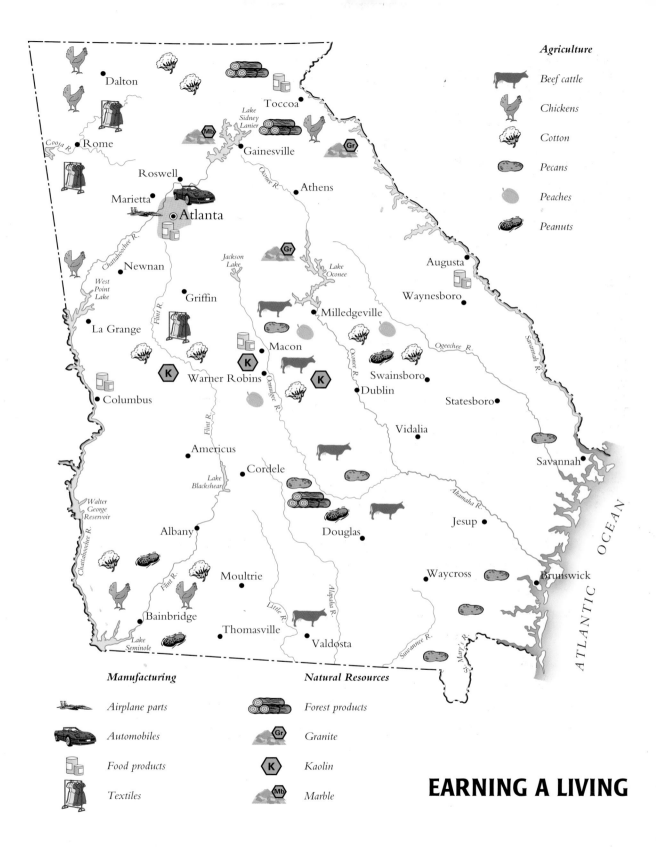

EARNING A LIVING

Agriculture

- Beef cattle
- Chickens
- Cotton
- Pecans
- Peaches
- Peanuts

Manufacturing

- Airplane parts
- Automobiles
- Food products
- Textiles

Natural Resources

- Forest products
- Gr Granite
- K Kaolin
- Mb Marble

Dalton
Rome
Coosa R.
Roswell
Marietta
Newnan
West Point Lake
La Grange
Columbus
Chattahoochee R.
Griffin
Flint R.
Warner Robins
Americus
Flint R.
Albany
Moultrie
Bainbridge
Lake Seminole
Thomasville
Little R.
Valdosta
Alapaha R.
Suwannee R.
Mary's R.

Toccoa
Lake Sidney Lanier
Gainesville
Oconee R.
Athens
Atlanta
Jackson Lake
Lake Oconee
Macon
Milledgeville
Oconee R.
Omulgee R.
Dublin
Swainsboro
Ogeechee R.
Cordele
Lake Blackshear
Walter George Reservoir
Chattahoochee R.
Douglas
Jesup
Waycross
Altamaha R.

Augusta
Waynesboro
Savannah R.
Statesboro
Vidalia
Savannah
Brunswick

ATLANTIC OCEAN

kettle by Atlanta pharmacist John S. Pemberton in 1886. It was sold as a medicine to relieve such common ailments as headaches, indigestion, and sluggishness. The secret formula for Coke has remained a closely guarded secret over the years. Charles Howard Candler, son of Asa Candler, who bought the business after Pemberton's death in 1891, recalled the time his father shared the secret formula with him: "No written formulae were shown. Containers of ingredients, from which the labels had been removed, were identified only by sight, smell, and remembering where each was put on the shelf. To be safe, father stood by me several times while I compounded these distinctive flavors."

Today, the formula for Coca-Cola resides in a safe-deposit vault in the Trust Company of Georgia, the bank that controls the company stock.

In the 1990s, Georgia became one of the leading states for jobs in high technology. These jobs include not only manufacturing computer parts but also computer-related services, communications services, and software development.

Sleek interstate highways and modern train lines link Georgia's towns and cities. Atlanta remains, as it was in Civil War days, the transportation hub of the state and the entire Southeast. It boasts the second-busiest airport in the nation—Atlanta Hartsfield International Airport.

GROWING AND SPRAWLING

For several decades, Atlanta has welcomed newcomers from rural areas and other states with open arms. This influx of new residents has

FIGHTING DISEASE ON THE FRONT LINE

If and when a cure for the deadly disease AIDS (Acquired Immunity Deficiency Syndrome) is found, the Centers for Disease Control and Prevention (CDC) in Atlanta will probably play a large role in finding it. Headquartered in Georgia's capital since 1946, the organization was formed to fight malaria and typhus, diseases that at the time threatened residents of the Deep South. Since then, the CDC's laboratories have researched and found ways to control and prevent polio, smallpox, Legionnaire's disease, and a host of other infectious diseases. Besides the challenging task of fighting disease, the CDC distributes public health information across the country and serves as a training center for health workers.

The CDC's weekly paper reported the first cases of AIDS in 1981. Six years later it announced the connection between the sometimes fatal disease Reyes Syndrome and aspirin in children. More recently it has taken aim at such chronic diseases as cancer and heart disease. With their successful track record, it is hoped that the dedicated medical workers at the CDC will be able to find better treatments for AIDS and other deadly diseases.

strengthened the state's economy and given the capital a modern, cosmopolitan atmosphere unknown elsewhere in the South.

But this growth has had its price. Today, Atlanta is one of the nation's largest metropolitan areas. It encompasses ten counties with a population of 3.1 million. From 1990 to 1998 the metropolitan population grew by 25 percent. The city's suburban sprawl has created the longest commute for workers of any city in the country—36.5 daily miles round trip, 16 miles farther than in Los Angeles, California.

And the city continues to sprawl. Every day more than fifty acres of green space in greater Atlanta are destroyed for new development. Once-rustic neighborhoods are now surrounded by shopping malls and commercial strips. "People who visited us five years ago say, 'I couldn't find your house,'" complains Julie Haley of Alpharetta. "The roads have all gotten wider, they've knocked down all the trees, there's a million shopping centers."

The state government is doing what it can to stop or at least slow the sprawl and improve the quality of life. Governor Roy Barnes

Georgia's freeways link country to city, but also tie up rush-hour traffic for hours.

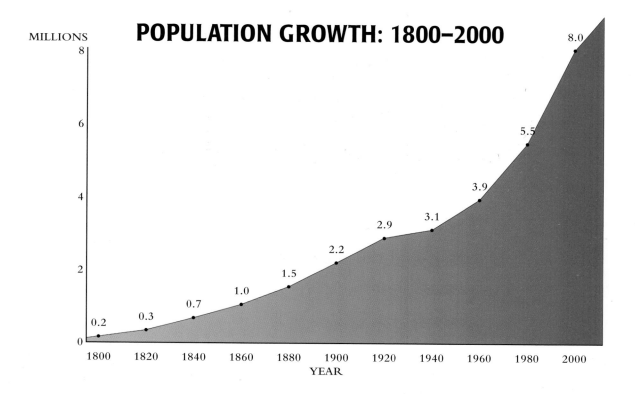

POPULATION GROWTH: 1800–2000

MILLIONS

YEAR

0.2 — 1800
0.3 — 1820
0.7 — 1840
1.0 — 1860
1.5 — 1880
2.2 — 1900
2.9 — 1920
3.1 — 1940
3.9 — 1960
5.5 — 1980
8.0 — 2000

created a new agency called the Georgia Regional Transportation Authority to extend the city's mass transit system to the suburbs and cut down on commuting cars, a major source of air pollution. "This whole process in regard to regional transportation has been to make sure we continued to grow and not stop it," Governor Barnes has stressed. "But it has to be growth in a planned sort of way."

How Georgia will grow and still meet the needs of both urban and suburban dwellers is a major issue for the state as it enters the twenty-first century.

4 PEOPLE AND PASTIMES

Georgia is a state that has reinvented itself time after time, from a land of plantation splendor to dirt poverty, from a segregated society to an integrated one. Georgia is, like Scarlett O'Hara, the heroine of the novel *Gone with the Wind*, a survivor. Whites make up 71 percent of the state's population and African Americans 27 percent. Hispanics, Asians, Pacific Islanders, and American Indians make up the remaining 2 percent of the population.

THE ISSUE OF RACE

While black Georgians are a minority statewide, they are the majority in some cities, including Atlanta, where two-thirds of the population is African American. Blacks hold many of the top positions in city government and business. Black dominance in the cities began in the 1970s, when many black Georgians began returning to their home state from the North as the state's job opportunities, economy, and race relations improved. But as African Americans moved into the cities, many white residents left for the suburbs. This "white flight" was particularly noticeable in Atlanta, which became ringed with white suburbs. Forsyth County, north of the city, has a lower proportion of African Americans than any other populous county in the nation. Intolerance in Forsyth County has diminished, however, since 1912,

The future looks bright for these African-American girls, thanks to improved race relations in recent years in Georgia.

when whites drove nearly all the blacks out of the area. But many blacks remain uncomfortable.

"I think people bend over backward to avoid any possibility of being unfair or racist," says lawyer Phillip Bettis, who was cochairman of a civil rights panel established in 1987. "We tell people, if you move here, you will be welcome, and you will be protected. But we haven't had many takers."

ETHNIC GEORGIA

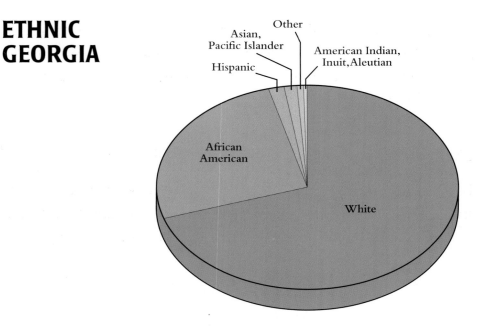

One of the few "takers," is Joseph Mosley, who lives in a white community and feels no prejudice against him. "I didn't come here to teach any lessons," he says. "But if my being here teaches some people about whether an African American can move into a community and still uphold the standards everyone is striving for, well, then let my presence be an example."

A more dramatic example of changing times occurred in 1997 in the Atlanta suburb of Stone Mountain, when Chuck E. Burris was elected the town's first black mayor. Stone Mountain was the scene of the revival of the Ku Klux Klan in 1915, and Burris lives in the house once owned by former mayor and Imperial Wizard of the National Knights of the KKK, James R. Venable. "There's a new Klan in Stone Mountain," Burris points out, "only it's spelled with a C: c-l-a-n, citizens living as neighbors. And I guess I'm the black dragon." Stone Mountain, which today is about half black, is a classic example of how many people's attitudes toward race have changed in the last generation.

GEORGIA CRACKERS AND YANKEE HONKERS

The Old South lives on in Georgia's rural areas, where a shared past and old traditions still loom large. Other Americans have sometimes looked down their noses at rural Georgians, calling them

Rural Georgians lead a quieter life than city folk.

crackers or rednecks. The term *cracker*, referring to ignorant, poor whites, may have originated from the way wagoners cracked whips over their oxen to make them move. *Redneck* refers to the fact that many rural Georgians work outside in the sun, so their necks are often sunburned. Carter Crittenden, an Atlanta investor who grew up in the small town of Shellman, has a more precise definition. "A redneck is someone who didn't graduate or maybe even go to high school and is a laborer," he explains. "They say a redneck is a mean, evil person. But I never met anyone like that growing up in Shellman. And I haven't met anyone like that today."

While many of Georgia's small towns have changed relatively little, its cities, especially Atlanta, have seen tremendous changes in the past few decades, as tens of thousands of northerners have moved in with new companies and businesses. Native Georgians have reacted to this influx of "Yankees" with good humor and a certain uneasiness. "Although I certainly understand somebody from the land of freeze and squeeze wanting to seek asylum here, I also fear I'm losing my city," wrote Georgia humorist Lewis Grizzard. "Will Southerners start dropping the last part of everybody's first name like the honkers [Northerners] do? . . . Will the automobile horn drown out the lilt of 'Georgia on My Mind'? Will grits become extinct? Will corn bread give way to the bagel?"

For their part, displaced northerners have their own misgivings about what they left behind. "We had to get used to everything fried," says Diane Rowe, who recently moved to greater Atlanta from Connecticut with her husband and daughter. "The traffic is bad and the air is polluted. There's some culture here, but we miss New York City and the theater."

Going down to the local grocery store is still a special event in small-town Georgia.

BRING ON THE BARBECUE!

If you like barbecued pork, southern style, the place for you is the Big Pig Jig, a barbecue competition and festival held every October in Vienna, about 150 miles south of Atlanta. The event draws more than 25,000 barbecue lovers and features a carnival, a parade, a hog-calling contest, and even a five-kilometer "Hog Jog" run.

But the main event of the festival is the barbecue championship. Teams of barbecuers compete in such categories as Whole Hog, Shoulder, Ribs, Stew, Sauce, and Chicken-Q. In 1998, winning teams sported such colorful names as the Sporty Porkers, the Milledgeville Misfits, the Sow Bellies, and the Low Country Longshots.

Whether you come to cook or just fill your belly, you'll agree the Big Pig Jig is one Georgia tradition made in hog heaven.

On the other hand, Rowe loves the little community they're in and the weather. "It only snowed this winter once and it melted by noon," she recalls. And as transplants, the Rowes have lots of company. "I'd say at least half of the people in our community of fifty-seven homes are not native Georgians."

EDUCATION

One thing that makes Georgia attractive to newcomers is the public education system. Georgia was a latecomer to public education. Before 1870, "public" schools charged tuition or operated under the generosity of plantation owners. Slave children received little or no schooling. Integration of schools, although mandated by the Supreme Court in 1954, was slow to come to Georgia. Black students first attended previously all-white schools in 1961, and full integration lagged in Georgia for another decade.

In more recent years, Georgia has proven to be a leader in education. In 1995, it became the first state to offer free preschool for all four-year-olds. "Pre-K has helped her mature socially," says Greselda McLin-Middleton of her daughter, "and it's really positive because of the multiracial mix of her classmates. . . . It's especially good with so many mothers in the workplace."

But other state education initiatives are not looked on as favorably by parents and the public. In 1998, school officials eliminated recess in all Atlanta public elementary schools. "We are intent on improving academic performance," claimed superintendent of schools Benjamin Canada. "You don't do that by having kids hanging on the monkey bars."

Georgia is in the forefront of public education in such areas as universal free preschool.

Other experts and parents disagree. They see recess as an important time for kids to learn how to get along with each other. "We have many latchkey kids who go home and lock the door until their parents get home," points out child development expert Olga Jarrett from Georgia State University. "Now if they can't mingle with other kids at school or at home, how are they going to learn to resolve conflict with their peers?"

Higher education is a top priority in Georgia. The state is home to more than one hundred four-year colleges, universities, and other institutes. The largest is the University of Georgia in Athens, which was founded in 1785 as the first state-chartered university in the United States. Emory University in Atlanta is perhaps the state's most prestigious private university. There is a long and proud tradition of all-black colleges in Atlanta that includes Morehouse College, which Martin Luther King Jr. attended, and Spelman College.

RELIGION

From the revival meetings of the early Methodist circuit riders to the foot-stomping, gospel-singing black congregations of today, religion has been a joyous and vital part of life in Georgia.

The early colony included a variety of Protestant sects, including the Church of England, Lutheranism, Presbyterianism, and others. The first Baptist church was not founded until 1772, but today the Baptists are by far the state's largest denomination. Methodism is the next most common church. This is not surprising, since Methodism's founder, John Wesley, accompanied James Oglethorpe to Georgia from England in 1735 and stayed there for two years as a missionary. Today, Georgia also has many Catholic churches and Jewish synagogues.

THE SPORTING LIFE

Georgians are great sports lovers—both as spectators and participants. Atlanta is home to eight professional sports teams. The most famous is baseball's Atlanta Braves. On April 8, 1974, in

Atlanta Braves pitcher Greg Maddux gets ready to hurl one over the plate. The Braves are one of several winning sports teams in the capital city.

Atlanta–Fulton County Stadium, Braves' slugger Henry "Hank" Aaron hit his 715th home run, breaking Babe Ruth's record for career homers. The Braves won the World Series for the first time in 1995.

Similar thrills were felt by football fans when the Atlanta Falcons, affectionately known as the Dirty Birds, made it into the Super Bowl for the first time in thirty-three years in 1998. "A chill went through me," recalls Falcon fan Dick West. "Tears got in my eyes. My wife came in and said, 'You all right?' And I was speechless. Then I got over it, and I began to holler. . . . I thought this day would never come." Unfortunately, the Falcons lost to the Denver Broncos.

Every April the Masters Golf Tournament brings the greatest golfers in the world to the National Golf Club in Augusta. The tournament was begun in 1934 by pro golfing great Bobby Jones.

With forty-five state parks and two national forests, Georgia is a great place to get outside. Whether hiking on the Appalachian Trail or racing rubber rafts down the Chattahoochee River, Georgians know how to enjoy the great outdoors. Trout fishing is popular in

This shelter being raised near the Appalachian Trail will be a resting place for the many hikers who walk along the trail each year.

the northern mountains, and hunting for deer, wild turkey, and duck is popular throughout the state.

THE ARTS—FINE AND FOLK

Culture is one of the jewels in the crown of the Empire State of the South. Atlanta is home to many cultural institutions. The Woodruff Arts Center houses the High Museum of Art, the Alliance Theater Company, and the Atlanta Symphony Orchestra, along with the 14th Street Playhouse and the Atlanta College of Art. Theaters, museums, and symphony orchestras abound in Georgia's large cities and towns.

In rural Georgia, another kind of art is thriving—folk art. Georgia's folk furniture, ceramics, and textiles are experiencing a boom among art collectors and museums. Georgia folk pottery is particularly popular, with its characteristic humor and eccentricity. A good example are face jugs, which bear expressive, and sometimes grotesque, human faces. "What's so unique about Georgia's folk art is that it's an ongoing and continuing tradition," explains Donald Peirce, curator of decorative art at Atlanta's High Museum. "It's very family oriented and a tradition that is handed down through families."

That's certainly true in the case of folk potter Marie Rogers, seventy-seven, of Meansville. Her husband, his father, and his grandfather were all potters. "When they'd leave the house to go to their regular jobs, I'd sit there and try and try," she says. "I was playing with them pottery wheels. Finally I got it and I was real proud of myself."

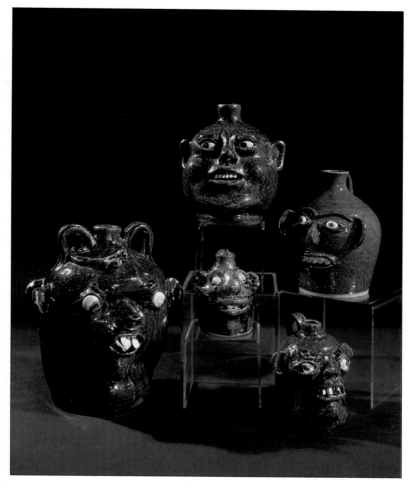

The grotesque and imaginative faces on these face jugs are an excellent example of Georgia folk art.

   Rogers is still proud of her pottery, which includes ring jugs of all kinds, busts, and barnyard animals such as roosters and pigs. "I just enjoy trying anything," she says with a laugh.

5 GREAT GEORGIANS

The Georgians who have made a mark on the nation have not always been understood or universally liked. That hasn't stopped them from achieving their goals with determination and courage.

THE FIRST GIRL SCOUT

Juliette Gordon Low spent half her life looking for a cause to live for, and when she finally found it, it became a mission. Daisy, as she was known as a girl, was born into a well-to-do Savannah family in 1860. She married a wealthy Englishman, William Low. From the start, the marriage was bad. On her wedding day, a grain of rice thrown by a well-wisher got lodged in Low's right ear and eventually made her deaf in that ear.

After her husband's death, Low became friends with Englishman Robert Baden-Powell, who had founded the Boy Scouts. Baden-Powell was interested in forming a similar group for young girls, which he called the Girl Guides, to teach "home-making and mother-craft." Low was enthusiastic about the idea, but she didn't stop there. She felt strongly that girls should be taught the same outdoor skills as the Boy Scouts were taught.

She returned to Savannah in 1912 and started the first American troop of Girl Scouts. Eight girls signed up, and she took them on a five-day camping trip. Low put all her energies and much of her

After returning to Savannah from England in 1912, Juliette Gordon Low (center) told a cousin that she wanted to do something "for all the girls of Savannah and all America and all the world." That "something" was the Girl Scouts.

money into the Girl Scouts of America. Under her guidance it grew from 8 girls to about 42,000 in 1920, the year she retired as the group's first president. When she died in 1927, Juliette G. Low was buried in her Girl Scout uniform. In her pocket was a telegram from the head of the organization that read: "You are not only the first Girl Scout but the best Girl Scout of them all."

THE GEORGIA PEACH

Ty Cobb holds the distinction of being both one of the greatest baseball players ever and one of the most disliked, even by his own teammates. Nicknamed the Georgia Peach early in his career, he was one peach who was anything but sweet.

Cobb was born in Banks County, Georgia, in 1886. His father, who had been both a schoolteacher and a state senator, was a stern taskmaster. When Ty decided on a baseball career against his father's wishes, the elder Cobb told him, "Don't come home a failure." These were words that Ty Cobb never forget. He spent the next twenty-five years working to be the very best in his sport.

Soon after signing with the Detroit Tigers in 1905, Cobb began

"Ty Cobb was a fascinating man," wrote one biographer. "He could graciously dine with bankers and presidents, yet he was vulgar, violent and despised by every player in the league, including his own teammates."

proving himself a superb hitter, an excellent outfielder, and a whiz at stealing bases. When he retired in 1928, he had a career batting average of .366. His 4,191 career hits remained the major league record for fifty-seven years, until Pete Rose of the Cincinnati Reds broke it in 1985. All in all, Cobb set forty-three major league season records, some of which remain unbroken to this day. Cobb was one of the first five players elected to the National Baseball Hall of Fame.

A great athlete, Cobb was less than a great human being. He was aggressive and mean-spirited on and off the field, even to his teammates. Baseball and shrewd investments made Cobb rich, but he was not happy. He did little in retirement but play golf and make enemies. Whatever people thought of Ty Cobb, they remained in awe of his baseball skills and his total commitment to the game. As he once told a sportswriter, "Baseball was one hundred per cent of my life."

THE LONELIEST WRITER

Few American writers have become successful so early in life as Carson McCullers, and few have led such sad lives.

Carson McCullers's first ambition growing up in Columbus, Georgia, was to be a concert pianist. At age seventeen she went to New York City to study at the Juilliard School of Music. On her second day in the city, she lost all her tuition money on a subway and gave up on Juilliard. Instead, she found part-time work during the day and attended writing classes at Columbia and New York Universities at night. She soon started writing stories, two of

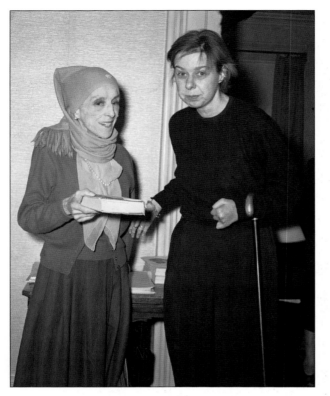

Writer Carson McCullers (right) had a sickly body but a healthy imagination. She is seen here with Danish writer Isak Dinesen.

which were published in magazines. In 1940, her first novel, *The Heart Is a Lonely Hunter*, was published to great acclaim. She was only twenty-three years old. The novel tells the story of a deaf-mute whose kindness and wisdom affect many people in a small southern town. The book's theme—loneliness that is only relieved by love— became central to all McCullers's work.

More novels and stories followed, including her best-known book, *The Member of the Wedding*. It is the story of Frankie, a misunderstood and rebellious adolescent girl who longs to share the life of her grown-up cousin who is about to be married. McCullers adapted the novel into a successful play, and it was later made into a popular movie.

SIDNEY LANIER—STATE POET

Sidney Lanier is perhaps Georgia's best-known and most-loved poet. Born in Macon, Lanier was a Confederate soldier and a prisoner in the Civil War. After the war, he pursued many careers—teacher, law clerk, English lecturer at Johns Hopkins University, and flutist. Lanier left Georgia and moved north in 1873 because Georgia's humid climate was hard on his ailing lungs. He rarely returned to Georgia, but he celebrated his home state and its natural beauty in some of his finest poems, including "The Marshes of Glynn," published in 1884. Here are some lines from it:

When the gray beach glimmering runs, as a belt of the dawn,
For a mete* and a mark
To the forest-dark:—
So:
Affable live-oak, leaning low,—
Thus—with your favor—soft, with a reverent hand.
(Not lightly touching your person, Lord of the land!)
Bending your beauty aside, with a step I stand
On the firm-packed sand,
Free
By a world of marsh that borders a world of sea.

*boundary

While her career thrived, McCullers's health was fragile. She suffered several strokes while still in her twenties and late in her life was confined to a wheelchair. She died in 1967 at age fifty. McCullers once noted that "a writer writes out of some inward compulsion to transform her own experience . . . into the universal. . . . Certainly I have always felt alone."

AUTHOR OF AN AMERICAN EPIC

Few best-selling novels have had the impact of *Gone with the Wind*, a saga of love and life in and around Atlanta before, during, and after the Civil War. Millions have thrilled to the star-crossed romance of Scarlett O'Hara and Rhett Butler, and millions more have seen the Hollywood movie based on the book.

Margaret Mitchell might never have written her famous novel if her husband hadn't encouraged her to do something constructive while she recovered from a broken ankle. Mitchell, who had previously been a reporter for the *Atlanta Journal*, was a lifelong resident of Atlanta. She decided to write a book about the city's proud past and spent ten years working on it. Published in 1936, *Gone with the Wind* was a sensation. More than a million copies were sold in just six months. It won Mitchell the Pulitzer Prize for fiction in 1937.

Fame and publicity kept Margaret Mitchell from her writing desk, and she never wrote another book. On a hot August day in 1949, the forty-eight-year-old author was struck by a car on a downtown street. She died five days later.

Civil rights leader Martin Luther King Jr. shares a quiet moment with his son Dexter.

MAN WITH A DREAM

"The only weapon we have . . . is the weapon of protest," Martin Luther King Jr. told his followers in Montgomery, Alabama, in 1955. In the hands of this civil rights leader, protest would become a powerful enough weapon to bring down a century of injustice and discrimination in the post–Civil War South.

King came from a family of powerful speakers. His father and grandfather had both been pastors at the Ebenezer Baptist Church in Atlanta, where Martin was born in 1929. He was a good student and entered Morehouse College at age fifteen. He became an ordained minister while still a student there and eventually became a pastor in Montgomery, Alabama.

Montgomery, like many southern cities at the time, was segregated. When a black woman, Rosa Parks, refused to sit in the back of a segregated bus with other blacks, she was arrested. King helped Montgomery's black community organize a boycott of city buses in response. The boycott drew national attention and ended with the Supreme Court ordering the buses to be integrated.

In 1957, King, by then a national figure, helped organize the Southern Christian Leadership Conference (SCLC) to fight segregation. Peaceful protest was the way to change society, King believed, and he led march after march. But his nonviolent approach was often met with violence by southern police and white supremacists. King's home was bombed, and he was arrested many times. On August 28, 1963, King took his cause to the nation's capital and delivered his famous "I have a dream" speech to a crowd of 200,000 people at the Lincoln Memorial. In 1964, King was awarded the Nobel Peace Prize for leading the nonviolent struggle for black equality.

King did not live to see his dream of an integrated, loving America. In 1968, he was assassinated in Memphis, Tennessee. His dream, however, did not die with him, and today America is a better place for his having lived.

SOUL SINGER

Macon, Georgia, has produced a number of gifted rock and rhythm-and-blues singers, including Little Richard and Ray Charles. It also

was home to the man many people call the greatest soul singer of the 1960s—Otis Redding.

Redding was born in Dawson, Georgia, in 1941 and sang in church choirs as a youth. While still in his teens, he made his first recordings, but found little success. A few years later, he got a job driving for a Macon singing group. One day he drove them to Memphis for an audition with Stax Records. After the group auditioned, they remembered that Otis sang too, and encouraged the shy young man to record one of his songs for Stax president Jim Stewart. Redding sang a slow, soulful ballad he had written called "These Arms of Mine." Stewart was impressed and released the record. It became a hit, the first of many hit records Otis Redding would make at Stax.

Redding's career was taking off when he set off on a tour of the Midwest in December 1967. One cold night his plane crashed into a frozen lake near the airport at Madison, Wisconsin. Redding and four members of his backup band were killed. Three days earlier he had recorded a wistful ballad, "(Sittin' on) The Dock of the Bay," a song he had cowritten. It quickly became the number-one record in America, Otis Redding's only chart-topper. He was twenty-six years old at the time of his death.

A PRESIDENT FROM PLAINS

When Jimmy Carter was nearing the end of his term as governor of Georgia, his mother asked him what he planned to do next.

"I'm going to run for president," he told her.

"President of what?" she replied.

"Momma, I'm going to run for president of the United States, and I'm going to win."

Few Americans outside of his home state had ever heard of Jimmy Carter when he declared his presidential candidacy in 1974. But Carter persisted in his mission with the same steely determination that he did everything in his life. He won the Democratic nomination and then in November 1976 defeated president Gerald Ford.

One of the few presidents never to have served in the nation's capital before being elected, Carter came to the White House with limited experience. "I spend about half the time being a student," he confessed during his first year in office. But he soon became a leader, especially in foreign affairs. He strengthened America's bonds with

"He burns out Secret Service agents," says Jimmy Carter's biographer Douglas Brinkley about Carter's life since the presidency. "They can't keep up with him."

China and helped negotiate a historic peace treaty between Israel and its former enemy, Egypt. In domestic affairs, Carter was less successful. The economy foundered during his administration. In 1980, he lost his reelection bid to Ronald Reagan.

Jimmy Carter returned to his home in Plains, Georgia, where he had been a peanut farmer. Since then, he has been one of the busiest and most productive ex-presidents in American history. He has helped negotiate several foreign crises, works as a volunteer and spokesperson for Habitat for Humanity, which builds homes for disadvantaged people, and has written more than a dozen books. In August 1999, Carter and his wife, Rosalynn, each received the Presidential Medal of Freedom for their good works. "Jimmy and Rosalynn Carter have done more good things for more people in more places than any other couple on the face of the earth," said President Bill Clinton during the ceremony.

MEDIA MOGUL

In a world of cautious corporate executives, Ted Turner is a colorful adventurer, whose gambles have made him rich and successful.

Robert Edward Turner III was born in Cincinnati, Ohio, in 1938. His father owned a billboard advertising company. When Ted was eight, the family moved to Savannah. Ted was a rebel whose high spirits survived a stretch at a military academy and prep school. He studied economics at Brown University in Rhode Island, where he excelled in debating, sailing, and partying. He was expelled twice.

In 1960, Turner joined his father's company. Three years later, twenty-four-year-old Ted took over the business. He not only made it a bigger success than ever, but also diversified the company. Against the advice of everyone around him, he bought two failing television stations. He used a clever billboard advertising campaign and innovative programming to turn the stations around. Then he bought two sports teams, the last-place Atlanta Braves baseball team and the Atlanta Hawks basketball team, partly so he could televise their games on his stations. The teams gradually became winners.

In 1976, he risked his growing empire on the new technology of cable television. One of his station's signals was beamed through a satellite in space and became Superstation TBS (Turner Broadcasting System). By 1978, it was seen in two million households. Soon after he launched the Cable News Network (CNN), the first twenty-four-hour all-news network, and bought MGM's library of more than three thousand old movies for more than $1 billion. Both gambles paid off handsomely. CNN changed the face of television news, and the movies filled the programming on two new Turner cable networks, Turner Network Television (TNT) and Turner Classic Movies (TCM).

Today, Turner is one of America's wealthiest men and one of its most generous. In 1997, he pledged $1 billion to the United Nations, one of the biggest individual donations ever made.

Known as the Mouth of the South, Ted Turner is notorious for his outspokenness on politics and social issues. But unlike some people, he has backed his words with actions.

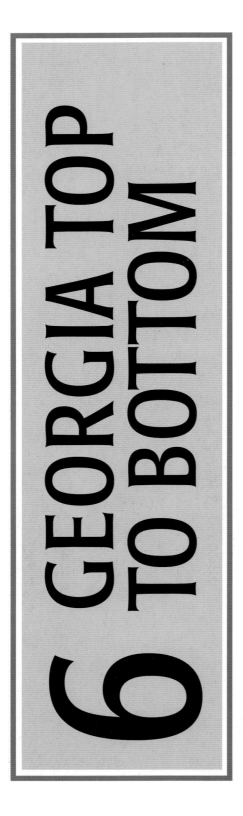

6 GEORGIA TOP TO BOTTOM

Georgia is a big state, chock-full of natural beauty, historic sites, and bustling cities. Let's take a tour of the state from top to bottom.

NORTHERN GEORGIA

Traveling south from Tennessee into the Peach State our first stop is the site of two major Civil War battles—the Chickamauga and Chattanooga National Military Park. Covering more than eight thousand acres of woods and battlefields, the park is the oldest and largest of its kind operated by the National Park Service. In September 1863, Union and Confederate troops met at Chickamauga Creek near the state line in a fierce battle that resulted in 28,000 casualties. The Chickamauga Visitors Center features a museum containing three hundred years' worth of American military shoulder arms. In Point Park visitors get a grand view of the countryside extending into Tennessee, Alabama, and Georgia. Point Park also houses an observatory and a restored Civil War home.

To the east, we find Chattahoochee National Forest, one of two national forests in the state. Chattahoochee boasts at least 135 species of trees, more than any other forest in North America. A few miles south lies Amicalola Falls, the highest falls in the state. This cold, crystal-clear mountain creek drops 729 feet in seven breathtaking cascades.

Cannons and monuments stand like quiet sentinels at the Chickmauga and Chattanooga National Military Park.

Farther south we come to the town of Rome, which like its namesake, Rome, Italy, is built on seven hills. In 1929, Italian dictator Benito Mussolini sent a bronze replica of a Roman statue to Rome's sister city in America. The sculpture, depicting the she-wolf that nursed the city's legendary founders, Romulus and Remus, still stands in front of Rome's city hall.

Moving south we enter the great city of Atlanta. Atlanta has so many treasures that it's hard to know where to begin. One of the most moving places to visit is the Martin Luther King Jr. National Historic Site. It includes the modest house on Auburn Avenue where King was born, and Ebenezer Baptist Church where both he and his father preached. At the King Center you can see the slain civil rights leader's white marble tomb, inscribed with words from his famous March on Washington speech: "Free at Last. Free at Last. Thank God Almighty I'm Free At Last." King's Nobel Peace Prize and other personal effects are on display in Freedom Hall.

Martin Luther King's tomb is one of the most moving places in all Atlanta.

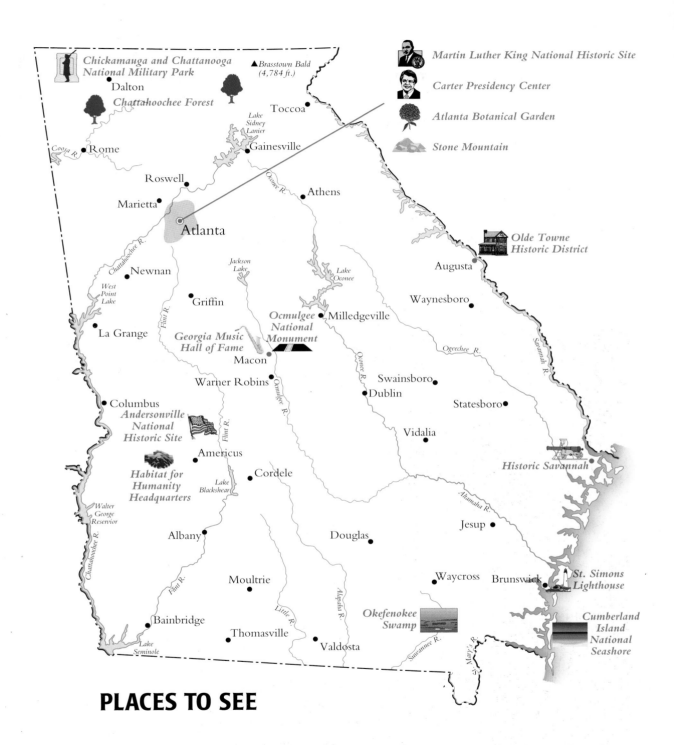

Chickamauga and Chattanooga National Military Park

▲*Brasstown Bald (4,784 ft.)*

Martin Luther King National Historic Site

Carter Presidency Center

Atlanta Botanical Garden

Stone Mountain

Dalton

Chattahoochee Forest

Lake Sidney Lanier

Toccoa

Coosa R.

Rome

Gainesville

Oconee R.

Roswell

Marietta

Athens

Atlanta

Olde Towne Historic District

Jackson Lake

Lake Oconee

Augusta

Chattahoochee R.

Newnan

Griffin

West Point Lake

Flint R.

Waynesboro

Ocmulgee National Monument

Milledgeville

Ogeechee R.

Savannah R.

La Grange

Georgia Music Hall of Fame

Macon

Swainsboro

Warner Robins

Ocmulgee R.

Dublin

Oconee R.

Statesboro

Columbus

Andersonville National Historic Site

Vidalia

Flint R.

Americus

Cordele

Habitat for Humanity Headquarters

Lake Blackshear

Altamaha R.

Historic Savannah

Walter George Reservoir

Chattahoochee R.

Albany

Douglas

Jesup

Moultrie

St. Simons Lighthouse

Waycross

Brunswick

Alapaha R.

Little R.

Okefenokee Swamp

Cumberland Island National Seashore

Bainbridge

Thomasville

Valdosta

Suwannee R.

Mary's R.

Lake Seminole

PLACES TO SEE

Equally impressive is the Carter Presidential Center, which includes the Museum of the Jimmy Carter Library, built to honor the only Georgian to become president. The Carter Center runs various international programs on human rights and conflict resolution.

When you're tired of museums and historic sites, you might spend an afternoon shopping and eating in the Buckhead section of Atlanta, which writer Florence Fabricant has called "the jewel of the city, an area of gracious homes, elegant hotels and shopping

TEN LARGEST CITIES

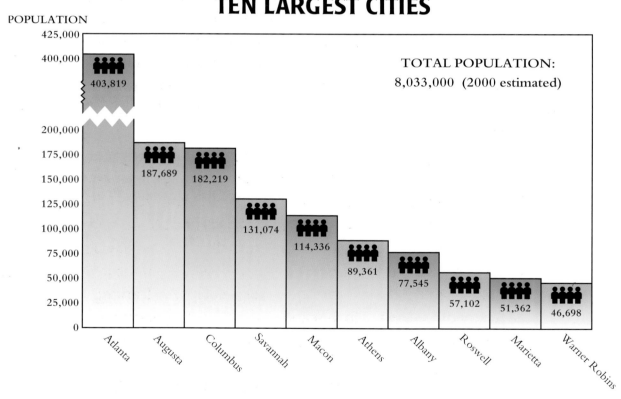

POPULATION

TOTAL POPULATION:
8,033,000 (2000 estimated)

Atlanta: 403,819
Augusta: 187,689
Columbus: 182,219
Savannah: 131,074
Macon: 114,336
Athens: 89,361
Albany: 77,545
Roswell: 57,102
Marietta: 51,362
Warner Robins: 46,698

centers, as well as some of the best restaurants." Liz Lane Porter, who lives with her husband and two children in Buckhead, sees it as the perfect place to raise a family. "The public elementary school is close enough for our kids to walk to," she explains. "There's a park nearby with bikers and joggers and moms pushing strollers." Atlanta, for her, is a city of greenery. "We've been more careful about keeping our trees than in some cities," she says.

If it's greenery you're looking for, you can hardly do better than the Atlanta Botanical Gardens in Piedmont Park. Its Fuqua Conservatory features many tropical and endangered plants, none rarer than the *Amorphophallus titanum* of Sumatra. The world's largest flowering plant, it has flowered only six times in cultivation in this country. Besides its size, the flower has another claim to fame: its horrible aroma. Tropical plants curator Ron Gagliardo describes the smell of its blossom as "a cross between a dead animal and a rotting pumpkin. You get used to it, but in the first few minutes [of blooming] it was a little nauseating even for me."

A more common but very intriguing plant grows in the town of Athens to the east. The white oak tree that stands in a town square is respectfully known as the Tree That Owns Itself. Many years ago the tree's owner deeded the tree ownership of itself and all the land within eight feet of its trunk. The original tree fell in a 1942 storm, but another has grown from one of its acorns on the same site. Athens is also home to Georgia's oldest institute of higher learning, the University of Georgia, which features the Georgia Museum of Art and the Collegiate Tennis Hall of Fame, which honors great college tennis players.

Farther east we enter beautiful Augusta, Georgia's second-oldest

STONE MOUNTAIN

Just east of Atlanta stands one of the most spectacular creations of nature and humankind—the Stone Mountain monument. Chiseled on this 300-million-year-old granite mountain are the Confederacy's three greatest heroes mounted on horseback—General Robert E. Lee, General Thomas "Stonewall" Jackson, and President Jefferson Davis. Spreading over an area 90 by 190 feet on the north face of the mountain, it is the world's largest sculpture.

This grand work was begun in 1923 but abandoned some years later. Work finally resumed and the sculpture was completed in 1970—fifty-four years after it was first conceived.

A hiking trail winds up to the mountain's summit, but less ambitious visitors can ride a cable car to the top or travel around the mountain on a locomotive from the Civil War era.

The Masters Golf Tournament was established in Augusta back in 1934 and has been held every spring since then, except for three years during World War II.

city, founded by James Oglethorpe in 1736. The gracious nineteenth- and early twentieth-century homes of the city's leading citizens have been lovingly restored in the Olde Town Historic District. Augusta was the state capital from 1786 to 1795, but it is better known today for the Masters Golf Tournament. Other international competitions that bring sports fans and athletes to Augusta include the Augusta Invitational Rowing Regatta and the Augusta Southern Nationals drag boat races.

CENTRAL GEORGIA

Macon, Georgia's fourth-largest city, is often called the heart of Georgia because it lies near the state's geographic center. It holds the distinction of being the only southeastern city that can trace its beginnings to a frontier fort, Fort Hawkins, built in 1806. The fort's remains still stand.

Home of poet Sidney Lanier and Wesleyan College, the first college chartered to grant degrees to women, Macon is now better known as the rock music capital of Georgia. The Georgia Music Hall of Fame contains photographs and memorabilia of some four hundred Georgia musicians and bands, including James Brown, the Marshall Tucker Band, and Macon's own Ray Charles and Otis Redding.

Near Macon is Ocmulgee National Monument, which contains one of the most spectacular arrays of Native American mounds and archaeological remains in the Southeast. A restored earth lodge built in 1015 by Indian farmers as a meetinghouse still has its original clay floor, wall benches, and partially standing walls.

Southwest of Macon along the Chattahoochee River lies Columbus, Georgia's second-largest city. The river has long been central to the city's life, and Columbus was a thriving river port until the coming of the railroad in the 1830s. Today, seven hydroelectric plants line the river, providing the power for Columbus's many factories. The Columbus Iron Works, which closed in 1964, produced the Confederate ironclad ship the CSS *Jackson/ Muscogee*, whose remains are on display at the Woodruff Museum of Civil War and Naval History.

Some 16,000 people are buried at the Andersonville National Cemetery. Andersonville was the worst of the Civil War prisons. "The swamp now is fearful," wrote one Union prisoner, "water perfectly reeking with prison offal [garbage] and poison. Still men drink it and die."

SOUTHERN GEORGIA

East of Columbus lies one of the grimmest reminders of the Civil War. It is not a battlefield, but a Confederate prison—Andersonville. The most notorious of all Civil War prisons, it once held over 33,000 Union prisoners of war, although it was built to accommodate only

10,000. Thousands of prisoners died of disease spread by filthy conditions and contaminated water. The national historic site includes the prison grounds, a national cemetery where more than 16,000 veterans and family members are buried, and the National Prisoner of War Museum, which examines prisoners' experiences in every war our country has fought in.

Just ten miles to the southwest is a reminder of the better side of human nature—the headquarters of Habitat for Humanity International, located in the town of Americus. Founded in 1976, Habitat for Humanity uses volunteers to build and renovate homes for needy people in the United States and abroad. To date, the organization has provided 65,000 homes for more than 300,000 people. The headquarters contains a museum and tour center and an international village featuring examples of houses in many different countries.

Heading eastward to the Atlantic coast brings us to Savannah. The state's oldest city served as the colonial and state capital until 1785. Savannah's rich heritage is alive in its historic downtown, where twenty-two of the twenty-four squares laid out by James Oglethorpe survive. Dotted with gently flowing fountains, majestic live oaks, and historic statues, the squares are a reminder of a quaint and simpler time.

Among the most famous of Savannah's many historic buildings are the Herb House, the oldest standing building in Georgia, built in 1734, and the Pirates' House, a seaman's inn built in the mid-1700s and used by author Robert Louis Stevenson as one of the settings of his classic adventure story *Treasure Island*. Near the Savannah River, bronze tablets memorialize the launching of the SS *Savannah*,

THE LITTLE WHITE HOUSE

In 1924, New York politician Franklin Delano Roosevelt, who had been stricken with the crippling disease polio three years earlier, paid a visit to the waters of Warm Springs, Georgia. For several months, he swam daily in the pool of warm mineral waters. The treatments he received helped restore Roosevelt's sense of well-being and confidence. He returned to politics and in 1928 was elected governor of New York. But he did not forget Warm Springs. He bought the springs and the land around it and set up the Georgia Warm Springs Foundation. It provided treatments for polio patients who couldn't afford them.

After Roosevelt was elected president in 1932, he spent so much time at his cottage at Warm Springs that it was called the Little White House. He was there on April 12, 1945, posing for his portrait, when without warning, he collapsed and died.

Roosevelt's cottage at Warm Springs is now a state historic site. Today, visitors walk from a memorial fountain to a museum dedicated to Roosevelt's life and achievements. It is a fine monument to both a great American and the special place where he found healing and comfort.

Savannah's Gingerbread House is one of the hundreds of historic homes in this colorful coastal city.

A visitor pauses to admire the greenery of a gigantic tree on one of Georgia's Golden Isles.

which in 1819 became the first steamship to cross the Atlantic Ocean, traveling from Savannah to Liverpool, England. Nearby, visitors can take a cruise on the *Savannah River Queen*, a replica of a stern-wheeler ship from the 1800s.

From Savannah it's a short journey to Georgia's famous Golden Isles along the Atlantic coast. While Saint Simons, Sea Island, Little

Saint Simons, and Jekyll Island are favorite destinations for vacationers, lesser-known Sapelo Island, the northernmost isle, has its own charms and treasures. Among its sights are the University of Georgia's Marine Institute and the impressive mansion built for tobacco magnate R. J. Reynolds in 1925. Perhaps most intriguing of all is Hog Hammock, a community of descendants of slaves who lived and worked on the Sapelo Plantation.

Southwest from the coast we come to Folkston, which lies at the east entrance to the six-hundred-square-mile Okefenokee Swamp, most of which is a wildlife refuge. Farther west near the Florida

border is the small town of Thomasville, which was a popular winter resort for wealthy northerners in the late 1800s. One of the most prominent of its winter cottages for the rich is the Lapham-Patterson House on North Dawson Street. Every room in this spacious 1884 mansion is a different shape. It was also one of the first homes in the area to have indoor plumbing and a gas lighting system.

This ends our top-to-bottom tour of Georgia—Peach State, Goober State, Empire State of the South. For millions of Georgians its best name is simply "home."

Most of the misty, mysterious Okefenokee Swamp is a wildlife refuge.

THE FLAG: *The left side of the state flag, which was adopted in 1956, displays the state seal against a blue background. The right side depicts the confederate battle flag.*

THE SEAL: *Adopted in 1914, the state seal shows a man holding a sword standing amid three pillars. This scene represents Georgians' readiness to defend the Constitution. On banners around the pillars are the words* wisdom, justice, *and* moderation *from the state motto.*

STATE SURVEY

Statehood: January 2, 1788

Origin of Name: Named after King George II of England

Nickname: Empire State of the South; Peach State

Capital: Atlanta

Motto: Wisdom, Justice, and Moderation

Bird: Brown thrasher

Flower: Cherokee rose

Tree: Live oak

Fish: Largemouth bass

Fossil: Shark tooth

Gem: Quartz

Insect: Honeybee

Brown Thrasher

Cherokee rose

GEORGIA ON MY MIND

This beautiful song was written in 1930, but it wasn't until Ray Charles performed it before the state legislature on March 7, 1979, that it was adopted as the official state song.

Words by Stuart Gorrell　　　　　　　　　　　　**Music by Hoagy Carmichael**

GEOGRAPHY

Highest Point: 4,784 feet above sea level, at Brasstown Bald Mountain

Lowest Point: sea level along the coast

Area: 58,930 square miles

Greatest Distance, North to South: 318 miles

Greatest Distance, East to West: 278 miles

Hottest Recorded Temperature: 113°F at Greenville on May 27, 1978

Coldest Recorded Temperature: −17°F in Floyd County on January 27, 1940

Average Annual Precipitation: 50 inches

Major Rivers: Alapaha, Altamaha, Chattahoochee, Chattooga, Flint, Ocmulgee, Oconee, Ogeechee, Satilla, Savannah, Withlacoochee

Major Lakes: Allatoona, Hartwell, Oconee, Seminole, Sidney Lanier, Sinclair, West Point

Trees: beech, birch, cedar, cypress, hickory, live oak, magnolia, maple, palmetto, pine, sweet gum, tupelo, yellow poplar

Wild Plants: crimson trumpet vine, daisy, honeysuckle, laurel, Queen Anne's lace, red sumac, rhododendron, saltgrass, violet

Animals: alligator, beaver, black bear, copperhead snake, deer, fox, muskrat, rabbit, raccoon, squirrel, water moccasin, wild boar

Birds: anhinga, blue jay, cardinal, catbird, dove, duck, egret, heron, marsh hen, meadowlark, mockingbird, quail, towhee, vulture, wood thrush

Fish: bass, bream, catfish, drum, eel, mullet, oyster, rainbow trout, shad, shrimp

Endangered Animals: amber darter, American peregrine falcon, Conasauga logperch, Coosa moccasinshell, Etowah darter, fat three-ridge (mussel), gray bat, Gulf moccasinshell, Indiana bat, Ochlockonee moccasinshell, oval pigtoe, ovate clubshell, red-cockaded woodpecker, shinyrayed pocketbook, southern acornshell, southern clubshell, southern pigtoe, triangular kidneyshell, upland combshell, West Indian manatee, wood stork

Manatees

Endangered Plants: American chaffseed, black-spored quillwort, Canby's dropwort, Florida torreya, fringed campion, green pitcher-plant, hairy rattleweed, harperella, large-flowered skullcap, mat-forming quillwort, Michaux's sumac, persistent trillium, pondberry, relict trillium, smooth coneflower, Tennessee yellow-eyed grass

TIMELINE

Georgia History

1400s Creek and Cherokee Indians live in present-day Georgia

1540 Spaniard Hernando de Soto passes through Georgia

1733 James Oglethorpe establishes Georgia's first permanent European settlement in Savannah

1763 The *Georgia Gazette*, the state's first newspaper, begins publication in Savannah

1775 The Revolutionary War begins

1788 Georgia becomes the fourth state

1793 Eli Whitney invents the cotton gin near Savannah

1828 Gold is discovered near Dahlonega, setting off America's first gold rush

1837 Atlanta is founded

1838 The Cherokee Indians are forced out of Georgia

1861 Georgia secedes from the Union; the Civil War begins

1864 Union general William Tecumseh Sherman burns Atlanta

1868 Atlanta becomes the state capital

1870 Georgia is readmitted to the Union; the state establishes a system of public schools

1917–1918 About 95,000 Georgians serve in World War I

1922 Georgian Rebecca L. Felton becomes the first female U.S. senator; WSB, the first radio station in the South, begins broadcasting in Atlanta

1941–1945 The United States participates in World War II

1943 Georgia becomes the first state to extend the vote to 18-year-olds

1948 WSB-TV, the South's first television station, goes on the air in Atlanta

1964 Georgian Martin Luther King Jr. receives the Nobel Peace Prize

1973 Atlanta citizens elect Maynard H. Jackson Jr. the first black mayor of a large southern city

1976 Georgian Jimmy Carter is elected president

1980 Atlanta resident Ted Turner founds Cable News Network (CNN), the first 24-hour all-news television station

1982 Georgia adopts its tenth and present constitution

1996 Atlanta hosts the summer Olympic Games

ECONOMY

Agricultural Products: apples, beef cattle, chickens, corn, cotton, eggs, hogs, milk, peaches, peanuts, pecans, soybeans, tobacco, watermelons

Manufactured Products: carpeting, fabric, food products, paints, paper products, pharmaceuticals, transportation equipment

Natural Resources: crushed stone, granite, kaolin, limestone, sand and gravel, shrimp

Business and Trade: banking, insurance, real estate, tourism, wholesale and retail trade

Shrimp

CALENDAR OF CELEBRATIONS

King Week Atlanta honors one of its greatest sons each January. For ten days, the city is filled with arts events and speeches commemorating Martin Luther King Jr.'s ideas about racial equality and harmony.

Augusta Cutting Horse Futurity and Festival Augusta hosts one of the world's top horse events each January. In addition to watching horse competitions, at this festival with a western feel you can also see displays of cowboy equipment and a cattle drive.

Winter Storytelling Festival Tales from around the world are brought to life at this Atlanta festival each January. When not listening to the spellbinding stories, you might watch jugglers or old-fashioned singers perform.

St. Patrick's Day Festival For a week each March, everyone in Savannah is Irish at the nation's second-largest celebration of Irishness. A half a million people show up for the parade, where even the dogs are dressed in green.

Cherry Blossom Festival The streets of downtown Macon burst into a riot of pink blossoms each March when the cherry trees bloom. To celebrate, arts and crafts booths, musicians, and festivalgoers fill the streets.

Vidalia Onion Festival Vidalia honors its famously sweet onions at this April event. There's an onion cook-off, an onion-eating contest, and lots of booths selling foods made with vidalias. If you don't like onions, you might still enjoy the airshow and the fireworks display.

Brunswick Harborfest Each May, Brunswick celebrates its history as a fishing port. Festivalgoers can tour a shrimp boat, see the blessing of the fleet, watch a water parade and powerboat races, and eat lots and lots of shrimp.

Civil War Encampment You can get a feel for what life was like for Civil War soldiers at this July event in Atlanta. Interpreters portraying people from both sides of the conflict tell stories to explain their experiences. Music and food from the time contribute to the Civil War atmosphere.

Aztec men at the Chehaw National Indian Festival

Sea Island Festival The traditional Gullah culture is honored on Saint Simons Island in August. You might eat traditional foods cooked over outdoor fires, learn traditional dances, or watch how fish nets and baskets are woven.

Big Pig Jig You'll eat your fill of barbecue at this celebration of the hog in Vienna each October. More than a hundred teams compete in the barbecue contest, but some people think the snorts and oinks of the hog-calling contest are more fun.

Mules Day More than 50,000 people show up in the tiny town of Calvalry each November to watch mule judging and a mule parade. This old-fashioned event also features a barbecue, a fish fry, a square dance, and syrup-making and tobacco-spitting contests.

Christmas in Savannah Old-time decorations enliven some of Savannah's most beautiful homes during the holiday season. You can tour some of these historic homes and also enjoy caroling and a candlelight tour of the city.

STATE STARS

Kim Basinger (1953–   ) is a popular actress known for her sultry roles. After beginning her career as a model, she broke into film in 1981. She was soon appearing in such movies as *Batman* and *Final Analysis*. Basinger earned her highest acclaim, winning an Academy Award for Best Supporting Actress, for her performance in *L.A. Confidential*. Basinger was born in Athens.

Kim Basinger

Julian Bond

Julian Bond (1940–   ), a civil rights leader and politician, was born in Tennessee and attended Morehouse College in Atlanta. He was one of the founders of the Student Nonviolent Coordinating Committee in 1960 and helped it become important in the drive to end segregation. He was elected to the Georgia House of Representatives in 1965, but the house refused to let him take his seat because he opposed the Vietnam War. The U.S. Supreme Court eventually ruled that this violated his right to free speech. He was finally seated in 1967. Bond served in the Georgia legislature until 1987.

James Brown (1928–   ), a native of Macon, is a soul singer whose high-energy shows earned him the nickname the Hardest Working Man in Show Business. Brown began his career in the late 1940s as a gospel singer. By the mid-1950s, he was focusing more on rhythm and blues. In 1956, he had his first big hit, "Please, Please, Please." Brown dominated the rhythm-and-blues charts throughout the late 1960s and early 1970s with songs such as "Papa's Got a Brand New Bag" and "I Got You." Brown was one of the first ten inductees into the Rock and Roll Hall of Fame.

James Brown

Jim Brown (1936–   ), one of the best running backs in football history, led the National Football League in rushing eight times in his nine-year career. As a running back, Brown had it all—speed, power, and agility. He was also remarkably sturdy and never missed a game because of injury. Brown, who spent his entire career with the Cleveland Browns, won the Most Valuable Player Award three times and was elected to the Pro Football Hall of Fame in 1971. He was born in Saint Simons Island.

Jim Brown

Asa Griggs Candler (1851–1929) established the Coca-Cola Company in 1892 after purchasing the business from pharmacist John Pemberton, who had developed the drink. Candler marketed Coca-Cola widely, putting it on murals, posters, and drinking glasses. He was also the first person to use coupons to lure customers. Candler quickly made Coca-Cola into one of the most successful businesses in the South. He retired from the company in 1915 and was elected mayor of Atlanta. He was born near Villa Rica.

Jimmy Carter (1924–   ), the thirty-ninth president of the United States, was born in Plains. He worked as a naval officer and a peanut farmer before turning his attention to politics. Carter served in the Georgia senate and as governor before being elected president in 1976. Since leaving office, Carter has helped negotiate several foreign crises and is widely respected for his charitable works, particularly with Habitat for Humanity, a group that builds housing for needy people.

Ty Cobb (1886–1961), a native of Narrows, was one of the greatest baseball players of all time. During his long career with Detroit, he established several records that still stand, including the highest career batting average at .366 and the most runs scored at 2,245. Cobb was famously mean and temperamental, but his talent was undeniable. He led the American League in steals during six seasons and won the league batting title nine years in a row. In 1936, he became one of the first five players elected to the National Baseball Hall of Fame.

Oliver Hardy (1892–1957), was one of the most popular comedians in film history as half of the Laurel and Hardy comedy duo. The pudgy Hardy and the thin Stan Laurel first teamed up in the 1927 short *Duck Soup*. In the more than 100 movies they made, each played a similar character. Laurel was always getting them into trouble, and the situation would get messier and messier until Hardy's volcanic temper finally exploded. Their films, including *Sons of the Desert*, *Babes in Toyland*, and *The Music Box*, remain favorites to this day. Hardy was born in Harlem, Georgia.

Oliver Hardy and Stan Laurel

Doc Holliday (1852–1887), who was born in Griffin, was a legendary gambler and gunfighter. He worked as a dentist in the East but moved west in 1872 because the dry climate was supposed to be better for his ailing lungs. There, his gunfighting became legendary. In 1881, he was involved in the famous gunfight at the O.K. Corral.

Charlayne Hunter-Gault (1942–   ) was one of two students who forced the University of Georgia to open its doors to African Americans. She was born in South Carolina but moved to Atlanta when she was nine. She wanted to be a journalist, but the University of Georgia, which was all-white at the time, had the only journalism school in the state. In 1961, she and another black student were admitted to the university. She eventually became a writer for the *New Yorker* and the *New York Times*, and a correspondent on television's *McNeil/Lehrer NewsHour*.

Bobby Jones (1902–1971), a native of Atlanta, is considered by some to be the greatest golfer ever. In 1926, he became the first player to win the U.S. and British Opens in the same year. All told, he won the U.S. Open four times, the British Open three times, and the U.S. National Amateur Championship five times. In 1934, he founded the prestigious Masters Golf Tournament.

Bobby Jones

Martin Luther King Jr. (1929–1968) was the preeminent civil rights leader of the 1950s and 1960s. King, who was born in Atlanta, was a Baptist minister. He first gained national recognition in 1955 for leading a bus boycott in Montgomery, Alabama, in protest over the city's segregated seating on buses. King, who was a powerful and mesmerizing speaker, is perhaps best remembered for his "I have a dream" speech, delivered in Washington, D.C., in 1963. King, who advocated nonviolent protest, received the Nobel Peace Prize in 1964. He was assassinated in 1968.

Little Richard (1932–   ) was the wildest of the early rock-and-roll stars, famous for his pounding piano, enthusiastic singing, and occasional screams. His outrageous performances and songs had a strong influence on later groups such as the Rolling Stones and the Beatles. In 1956, Little Richard had his first hit with "Tutti Frutti," a song with nonsense lyrics but whose good-natured exuberance has made it a classic. He soon had hit after hit, including "Long Tall Sally" and "Good Golly, Miss Molly." In 1986, Little Richard became one of the original members of the Rock and Roll Hall of Fame. He was born in Macon.

Little Richard

Crawford Long (1815–1878) was a doctor who is credited with performing the first operation using ether as an anesthesia, which was a huge advance in surgery. Ether has a strong smell and causes people to lose consciousness when they inhale it. In 1842, Long gave a patient ether before removing a tumor. Within a few years, ether had become common in the operating room and remained so for a hundred years. Long was born in Danielsville.

Juliette Gordon Low (1860–1927), a native of Savannah, founded the Girl Scouts of America. Low was a friend of Robert Baden-Powell, who founded the Boy Scouts. Low organized a troop of Girl Scouts in Savannah in 1912. She served as the president of the Girl Scouts in America until 1920.

Carson McCullers (1917–1967), who was born in Columbus, wrote novels that drew on her southern childhood. Her books, which are usually set in small towns, are filled with loneliness. Her most famous novels include *The Heart Is a Lonely Hunter* and *The Member of the Wedding*.

Willie McTell (1901–1959), one of the greatest of all blues singers and guitarists, was renowned for his guitar mastery and warm voice. McTell, who was born blind, began playing harmonica and accordion as a child. He eventually switched to guitar and earned acclaim for the delicacy and agility with which he played the 12-string. He began recording in 1927 and soon laid down some of his most famous songs, including "Statesboro Blues." McTell was born in Thomson.

Willie McTell

Johnny Mercer (1909–1976) was a songwriter, most famous for writing the lyrics for many hit songs in movies. He wrote the words to such

)

classics as "I'm an Old Cowhand" and "Jeepers Creepers." Over his long career he won three Academy Awards, including one for "Moon River" from the film *Breakfast at Tiffany's*. Mercer was a native of Savannah.

Johnny Mercer

Jessye Norman (1945–   ) is an opera singer, famous around the world for her rich, emotional voice and commanding stage presence. Norman, who was born in Augusta, first gained recognition when she won a voice competition in Germany in 1968. She made her operatic debut the following year and was soon filling opera houses across the globe. Today, she has a reputation as one of the world's most versatile and knowledgeable opera singers.

Jessye Norman

Flannery O'Connor (1925–1964) was an acclaimed fiction writer whose novels and stories typically have dark humor and grotesque characters. Her work, such as the novel *Wise Blood* and the short story collection *A Good Man Is Hard to Find*, are also strongly influenced by O'Connor's Roman Catholicism. For the last decade of her life, O'Connor suffered from lupus, a crippling disease that kept her in bed most of the time at her home in Milledgeville.

Ma Rainey (1886–1939), who was known as the Mother of the Blues, had a powerful, brooding singing style that influenced many younger performers. By the time she cut her first record in 1923, Rainey was already one of the world's most famous blues singers and had been performing in front of audiences for more than 20 years. She made such songs as "C.C. Rider" and "Bo Weevil Blues" into classics. Rainey was born in Columbus.

Otis Redding (1941–1967), a singer known for his grainy voice and emotional ballads, was born in Macon. Redding began recording in 1960 and soon had such hits as "Try a Little Tenderness" and "Mr. Pitiful." His most famous song, "(Sittin' on) The Dock of the Bay," was released after he died in a plane crash. It earned him two Grammy Awards and was his only song to hit number one on the pop charts.

Jackie Robinson (1919–1972) broke the color barrier in Major League baseball. Robinson was a remarkable all-around athlete. At the University of California at Los Angeles, he became the first student to earn varsity letters in four sports—football, basketball, baseball, and track. When Robinson began playing professional baseball, the Major Leagues did not allow black players. So instead, he played with the Kansas City Monarchs of the Negro Leagues. In 1947, he joined the Brooklyn Dodgers, becoming

the first black player in the majors. His aggressive baserunning and graceful fielding helped the Dodgers win the National League pennant, and he was named Rookie of the Year. In 1962, he became the first African-American player inducted into the National Baseball Hall of Fame. Robinson was born in Cairo.

Jackie Robinson

Sequoya (1770?–1843) invented the Cherokee alphabet. Born in Tennessee, Sequoya later settled in Cherokee County, Georgia, where he worked as a silversmith and trader. In an effort to preserve Cherokee culture, he developed an alphabet consisting of 86 characters, which represented every syllable in the Cherokee language. Soon books and newspapers were being published in Cherokee. Never before had a written language been developed for an American Indian language.

Clarence Thomas (1948–   ) is the second African American to the serve on the U.S. Supreme Court. Thomas began his career as an assistant attorney general for Missouri. While serving as the chairman of the Equal Employment Opportunity Commission, he became known for his conservative beliefs. Thomas, who was appointed to the Court in 1991, was born in Savannah.

Ted Turner (1938–   ) is one of the most famous and successful business-people in America. Turner, who was born in Ohio, got his start when he took over his family's billboard business in 1963. In 1970, he bought a television station in Atlanta, which he eventually turned into WTBS, the first "super-

station," which used satellites to send programming to cable systems around the country. This innovation fostered the spread of cable television. In 1980, Turner founded Cable News Network (CNN), the first 24-hour all-news television station. Turner also owns the Atlanta Braves baseball team, the Atlanta Hawks basketball team, and the Atlanta Thrashers hockey team. In 1997, he made headlines when he pledged $1 billion to the United Nations, one of the largest charitable donations in history.

Alice Walker (1944–   ) writes books about the hardships faced by black women, particularly in earlier times. Her best-known work, the novel *The Color Purple*, was published in 1982 and won a Pulitzer Prize and an American Book Award. More recently, she has published *In Search of Our Mothers' Gardens*, a collection of essays and speeches about her experiences as a black woman in America. Walker was born in Eatonton.

Alice Walker

TOUR THE STATE

Chattooga Wild and Scenic River (Clayton) Float down a river though spectacular gorges filled with lush scenery, rocky outcrops, and refreshing waterfalls.

New Echota State Historic Site (Calhoun) In 1825, the Cherokee Nation established a capital at New Echota. Today, you can visit the old council house, which has been restored, along with their courthouse and a log store from the 1830s. The site also includes the shop where the first Cherokee newspaper, the *Cherokee Phoenix*, was printed in 1828.

Callaway Gardens (Pine Mountain) Hike down trails past luxurious flowering plants, enter a glass conservatory where a thousand butterflies will flutter around your head, and let your imagination run wild at the topiary garden, where plants are cut into fanciful shapes such as the Mad Hatter.

Paradise Gardens (Summerville) Folk artist Howard Finster created this unique garden filled with sculptures made of aluminum foil and old bicycle parts.

Brasstown Bald (Helen) Climb a steep trail to the top of Georgia's highest peak for a spectacular view in every direction. You can see four states from the top.

National Science Center's Fort Discovery (Augusta) At this high-tech museum, you can feel what it's like to walk on the moon and then explore nearly 300 other interactive exhibits.

Dahlonega Gold Museum (Dahlonega) This museum is housed in the oldest public building in northern Georgia. Inside, you'll see exhibits of gold coins and nuggets and mining tools, along with displays about Appalachian culture.

Amicalola Falls State Park (Dahlonega) At this park, you can admire fabulous falls that drop 729 feet and wondrous views of the Blue Ridge Mountains.

Cloudland Canyon State Park (Trenton) Outdoors lovers won't want to miss the hike through thick forests, past dramatic waterfalls, and up to an extraordinary view in one of Georgia's most scenic areas.

High Museum of Art (Atlanta) This eye-catching building contains four stories of art, from ancient pottery to contemporary painting.

Atlanta History Center (Atlanta) In the history museum, you can learn about the civil rights movement and southern culture. But the center also includes a grand early-20th-century house, with elaborate gardens and a working farm built in the style of the 1840s, where reenacters perform tasks such as sheepshearing and weaving.

Martin Luther King Jr. National Historic Site (Atlanta) This site includes King's birthplace, the Ebenezer Baptist Church, where he was a pastor in the 1960s, and his gravesite.

Stone Mountain (Stone Mountain) The largest relief sculpture in the world depicts the Confederate heroes Jefferson Davis, Robert E. Lee, and Stonewall Jackson.

Ocmulgee National Monument (Macon) At this site, you can see exhibits and artifacts covering 12,000 years of Indian settlement. Trails lead visitors around nine ceremonial mounds built by Indians, including the Great Temple Mound, which is more than 40 feet high. You can also see a restored earth lodge that would have been a typical meeting place.

Georgia Music Hall of Fame (Macon) You'll see and hear all about Georgia's varied musical history, from James Brown to Johnny Mercer, at this museum. It even has areas designed to look like a jazz club, a church, and a rock-and-roll record store, so you can get a feel for where the music came from.

Andersonville National Historic Site (Andersonville) This Confederate military prison was built to house 10,000 prisoners but held as many as 33,000. On a visit to the prison, you can see the escape tunnels prisoners dug and diaries and photographs that bring the prisoners' stories to life. More than 17,000 Union soldiers are buried at the Andersonville National Cemetery.

Davenport House (Savannah) The movement to save Savannah's famous architecture began in the 1950s when a group of citizens got together to preserve this lovely house built in 1820. Today you can tour the home, which is filled with antiques.

Okefenokee Swamp (Folkston) The dark brown waters and islands in this sprawling swamp are home to lots of animals, including alligators and black bears. A walk along boardwalks past cypress trees covered in moss will take you into this unusual landscape.

Saint Simons Lighthouse (Saint Simons Island) Climb to the top of this 104-foot lighthouse for a wonderful view. The light has been in operation since 1872.

Cumberland Island National Seashore (Saint Marys) Only 300 visitors a day are allowed into this preserve so that the island will remain pristine, able to support the loggerhead turtles, bobcats, and wild horses that live there.

FUN FACTS

Each year Georgia produces 1.1 billion square yards of carpeting. That is
enough to wrap a 12-foot-wide strip of carpet around Earth four times.

The first golf course in the United States was laid out in Savannah in 1794.

The Cyclorama Building in Atlanta contains the largest mural in the world.
This painting, which is 358 feet long, shows the Battle of Atlanta during
the Civil War.

FIND OUT MORE

Want to know more about Georgia? Check the library or bookstore for these titles.

GENERAL STATE BOOKS

Ladoux, Rita C. *Georgia*. Minneapolis, MN: Lerner Publications, 1996.

Masters, Nancy Robinson. *Georgia*. Chicago: Children's Press, 1999.

SPECIAL INTEREST BOOKS

Beatty, Patricià. *Be Ever Hopeful, Hannalee*. Mahwah, NJ: Troll Associates, 1991.

Buffington, Perry, and Kim Underwood. *Archival Atlanta: Electric Street Dummies, the Great Stonehenge Explosion, Nerve Tonics, and Bovine Laws. Forgotten Facts and Well-Kept Secrets from Our City's Past*. Atlanta, GA: Peachtree Publishers, 1996.

Fradin, Dennis Brindell. *The Georgia Colony*. Chicago: Children's Press, 1990.

McKissack, Patricia. *Martin Luther King, Jr.: A Man to Remember*. Chicago: Children's Press, 1984.

Perdue, Theda. *The Cherokee*. New York: Chelsea House, 1989.

Schraff, Anne E. *Jimmy Carter*. Springfield, NJ: Enslow Publishers, 1998.

VIDEOS

Atlanta Cyclorama: Battle of Atlanta. 30 mins., Finley-Holiday Film Corp.

Atlanta's Olympic Glory. 210 mins., PBS Home Video.

INTERNET

State of Georgia Home Page
   http://www.state.ga.us

Georgia in the Civil War
   http://www.cherokeerose.com

Georgia Travel
   http://www.excite.com/travel/countries/united_states/georgia

INDEX

Page numbers for charts, graphs and illustrations are in boldface.